STORYTELLING and STORY-READING in EARLY YEARS

HOW TO TELL AND READ STORIES TO YOUNG CHILDREN

MARY MEDLICOTT

Jessica Kingsley *Publishers*
London and Philadelphia

First published in 2018
by Jessica Kingsley Publishers
73 Collier Street
London N1 9BE, UK
and
400 Market Street, Suite 400
Philadelphia, PA 19106, USA

www.jkp.com

Library of Congress Cataloging in Publication Data
Names: Medlicott, Mary, author.
Title: Storytelling and story-reading in early years : how to tell and read
   stories to young children / Mary Medlicott.
Description: London ; Philadelphia : Jessica Kingsley Publishers, 2018. |
   Includes index.
Identifiers: LCCN 2017058179 | ISBN 9781785922985 (alk. paper)
Subjects: LCSH: Storytelling. | Storytelling in education. | Early childhood
   education.
Classification: LCC LB1042 .M38 2018 | DDC 372.67/7--dc23
LC record available at https://lccn.loc.gov/2017058179

British Library Cataloguing in Publication Data
A CIP catalogue record for this book is available from the British Library

ISBN 978 1 78592 298 5
eISBN 978 1 78450 604 9

Printed and bound in Great Britain

Contents

1

THE IMPORTANCE OF STORY

Stories are all around us. They're in books and paintings, on TV and in films, in our dreams and day-dreams and in our conversations. Where would we be without them?

Imagine: It's Friday evening. You get together with friends for a quick drink before the weekend. Almost immediately, you're hearing a story. What happened when one friend's car broke down at midnight on the way home from a visit to her mother? What happened when another friend's child was terribly sick in the middle of the night? What happened when a third friend's cat went missing for four whole days? It's all very absorbing. One story sparks off another; it's the stuff of life but you probably don't normally ask yourself what life would be like without it.

Then it's Saturday night. You go to the cinema with your partner. The film you both wanted to see is a thriller. You're on the edge of your seat. Can you bear it? When you come out, you're talking about it. What was actually going on – remember? – when those two robbers were talking in that bar? Was she really in love with him by then? It's funny how much we take for granted. If films had never been invented, what would we do on a Saturday night?

By now, it's the middle of the week, Wednesday morning. You've had to take time off work. There's a family funeral you've got to attend. Everyone present is sad but there's a lot of good humour too. Grandma was old, she'd had a good life, and at the tea and sandwiches after the service, you all stand around and remember. You recall those times when you were all children and Grandma would astonish you and make you laugh with those tales of her growing up. You remember when you were teenagers and she never minded when you dyed your hair, she liked it. You remember once when she got furious because one of her neighbours had kicked her cat.

EVERYDAY TALES

All this talking is part of storytelling. It's the informal part, the stuff of ordinary everyday living, and it's well worth thinking about how our lives would be if it never occurred. Of course, for some people, not much of it does. People isolated by mobility problems, loss of family and friends or lack of money. People with depression, hearing loss or serious illness. People who've been obliged to move home or country and, perhaps because of language problems, haven't made any friends where they live now. Or people who are terribly shy. Besides, it's not everyone who is able to tell their stories even if they've got someone to tell them to. I remember one young mother on a storytelling course I was running. Towards the end of the term, she reported feeling very moved. She told me why. Before she came on the course, she said, her husband had never really said anything about his life before he met her, his childhood or growing up days. She and their children knew little about him. Now, responding to all the different kinds of stories she'd passed on to him from the course, he'd started talking, telling them things. They were learning much more about him. His wife felt grateful for the change.

TRADITIONAL TALES

Our life stories are vital. We wouldn't be human without them. But in the vast store of the world's stories, they form only one department. Others are comprised of the myths and legends, the folk tales and fairy tales, tall tales, jokes and riddles that people have shared in all the different parts of the world where human beings have lived going back to the beginnings of spoken language. It can be daunting even to think about it. Ancient Greek stories of the gods and goddesses. Old Norse sagas of mighty heroes. The Arabian Nights from the Middle East, the Mahabharata from India, the Mabinogion from Wales. Tales from the Americas, Iceland, Russia, the South Sea Islands, Africa, you name it: every part of the world has its stories. Some, such as the folk tales that were collected and published in 19th-century Germany by the Brothers Grimm, will be more familiar to more of us in the West. Others will remain outside our consciousness. Yet insofar as they've been passed on, whether in published or oral form, they continue to affect the cultures of the world as these exist today. Poets, novel writers and film-makers will have been influenced by them. So will the creators of children's computer games.

TALES WE CREATE

Stories we create for ourselves form another important section in the immeasurable world of storytelling. It's probably not a branch of storytelling that most people think of as having anything at all to do with them. Isn't making up stories what authors do, novelists and children's book writers and people like that? Yes. But it's also what the dreamers among us do when we imagine different lives for ourselves – how we might meet the love of our life and settle down in a lovely old house in the country with a dog and some cats – and oh, how about some children? Or how about our career ambitions – how we might get to run a bookshop one day or maybe even write a best-seller? And what about that strange dream you had last night? Where did that come from? Didn't it come from somewhere inside you?

I could go on. Even as we refer to our everyday tales of our own lives, it's possible to make a connection with history-writers and how they form our knowledge of the past. Digging into the archives of recorded events, researching previously unrecorded aspects of them, they have their own special understanding of the importance of story.

WHY STORIES ARE IMPORTANT

This book deals with the importance of stories for the full range of early years children with particular focus on three- to five-year-olds. It will cover two different ways of passing on stories, namely oral storytelling (telling a story without a book) and story-reading (reading a story from a written text, though perhaps with some rewording or ad-libbing). Yet, even as growing young children are at the centre of the book's concerns, the book itself must inevitably be addressed to the adults in their lives. It is written for people who work with children – teachers, nursery nurses, special assistants, speech and language specialists, psychotherapists, lunchtime assistants and supervisors – and also parents, foster parents and carers. For the concern of the book is how we as adults can help to give children the joyous and ever-expanding familiarity with stories that will form a positive basis for their development as human beings.

LEARNING AND DIGESTING

For a start, stories give a firm basis for the learning of language: stories normally (though not always) employ words, some of which might be new to an early years audience. Yet those words always come in a context, a framework which offers its own clues to the children who hear them as to what the words mean and how they are used. Then again, stories teach shape: they have beginnings and endings and middles. Shapes are useful because they give patterns and patterns are useful because they help us to understand what happens to us. Besides, the shapes of stories are more than architectural. They come with content, which includes emotions, and we all have to work hard to understand our own emotions let alone those of other people. Further to all of that, all stories are some kind of journey. Experiencing the journey, however long or short, involves discovering that, after it has started, it will sooner or later have an end. This discovery is highly productive for all kinds of things in the rest of life. Lessons, mealtimes, sitting on buses: accepting that stories have beginnings and ends teaches you about getting through time and, by the by, how to look out for something that might interest you along the way.

THE VALUE OF STORIES

Becoming aware of the value of stories is essential for anyone who works or lives with children. Children need things that help them to understand what is going on in their own lives: basic things such as happiness and sadness, difficulties with engaging with parents and teachers, siblings and friends. Children also need things that engage them, make them laugh, awaken their imagination. All these can be gained from stories. And that's where the ways in which you offer stories to children become so important. Stories are like food for children. But you can't shove food down children's throats. Stories have to be offered to children in ways they can cope with and also enjoy. Stories are not a punishment, not something to be endured, and they shouldn't be surrounded with instructions: 'Sit still. Sit up. Listen.' Stories need to be communicated in the spirit of discovery which makes them feel like an adventure. They also need to be communicated in the spirit of creating relationships. As pioneer storyteller Eileen Colwell (1980, p.3) described it, 'When storyteller and child meet, life is enriched for both by the sharing of a story. To have laughed together, shared excitement or sadness, experienced wonder and emotion, establishes a mutual feeling of warmth and comradeship, an experience worth all that it may cost in time and energy.'

WHAT THIS BOOK OFFERS

What this book offers is an opportunity to think about all the many aspects of how we can communicate stories to children. It offers suggestions on what kinds of stories might be best for children across the early years age range. It offers advice on how these stories might be presented both to a child on her or his own and to children in groups. It offers suggestions about how early years staff can prepare themselves for delivering their stories, whether through books or through oral telling. It talks about props and how these can be selected and used to add to the enjoyment and understanding of stories. Then it goes on to discuss how staff can help each other in regard to delivering the stories, how this can relate to parents and how these elements can be involved in building an overall strategy for dealing with stories in any early years setting.

MY PERSONAL EXPERIENCE

Where the book offers something fresh is that it deals both with story-reading and oral storytelling. As someone who has done a great deal of both, I have considerable experience of the links between them and the differences too. My first experience of both was during four years' part-time work on a scheme being run at that time in Brixton in South London where I live. The Lambeth Libraries Storytelling Scheme was highly innovative and it involved two different types of work. One was as a story reader going round under-fives groups in the borough on a regular basis to deliver story sessions. The other involved telling stories without using books to children of all ages who turned up for sessions on holiday schemes in the borough. The work was very part-time, not many hours per week and certainly not much pay. But from the very beginning, it seemed to offer me a remarkable opportunity to find out at first hand what kind of stories children respond to. For some years previously, I'd been working as a freelance journalist and my regular work had included reviewing children's books for a variety of newspapers and magazines. Alas, when you're reviewing books for children, you're not writing for the children themselves. You are writing for their teachers and parents. The Lambeth scheme would, I thought, provide a chance to discover for myself what children do and don't like.

I was right. Working for the Lambeth Libraries Story-telling Scheme (sadly long since defunct because of lack of funding) taught me a very great deal. It taught me about young children and how to get and keep their attention. It taught me about choosing which stories to select from among the huge variety of available picture books. It also taught me a lot about the people who work with young children. One result was completely unexpected. The realisation that books themselves do not speak and that you have to find ways to give them a voice made me learn about presenting stories to children. It also led me into realising how useful it could be to pass this on to other adults. There was, I found out, a big need for this. Story-reading and storytelling are hugely important but not much discussed among the adults who live and work with the children.

After leaving the Lambeth scheme, I began to develop a new career as an oral storyteller. A large part of my subsequent work was in education, working with children in nurseries, primary and secondary schools, and also with their teachers and carers. In Lambeth I'd already discovered the links and differences between story-reading and storytelling. Now, as an oral storyteller, I also became what I might describe as a proselytiser, someone who felt very keen to spread the word about oral storytelling and how vital it can be. Along with the many colleagues who also became part of what we'd now describe as the Storytelling Revival, I felt I wanted to encourage others to do it too, whether as fellow professionals or in their own working or personal lives. Storytelling, it seems true to say, had been dying out. Now we wanted others to experience the extraordinary atmosphere of hearing stories told 'by word of mouth', perhaps by someone sitting quietly in a chair using words alone, perhaps with action and music as part of the telling.

I shall certainly do my share of proselytising in this book. However, I shall not do it by downgrading the act of story-reading. Story-reading and oral storytelling provide somewhat different kinds of experience. Both are hugely important for young children and there are many common issues in regard to both types of activity. How to choose a story, how to prepare it, how to get and keep children's attention to it and how often to tell it: all are crucial whether you are reading or telling. But those are just the beginning. Beyond are the wider issues of how you embed the stories in children's lives, how you can create interesting activities that relate to the stories and at the same time assist children in their language and social development. In a way, it's like being a cook. Beyond the question of the particular dish you're going to serve this evening – its particular ingredients, the method of cooking and the time that will be needed – are all those other issues we read so much about today. What is your overall diet of which this particular recipe is part? Is it doing you good? Is your choice of ingredients healthy, for yourself, for any others who are going to eat the food you serve and for the wider world?

When I was working all those years ago on the Lambeth Libraries Storytelling Scheme, I came to realise that one major factor in the background of the scheme was not being given due attention. This was the people who regularly worked with the children. What did they think was going on? Did they like what their visiting story readers did or did they think they could do it better? Would they have liked to get more involved? Would they even have liked some help to improve their own performance? Questions such as these led to my later interest in what you might call staff training except that, to me, staff training in working with stories should always be as much about opening up to the experience of the staff concerned as about delivering instruction.

HOW WE ADULTS CAN HELP EACH OTHER

A running theme in this book is how adults in any early years setting can help each other in the job of delivering stories to children. Can more experienced adults assist people new to the work by discussing what stories work best and how to make those stories work? If one member of staff is experienced in the oral telling of stories, could she or he help others to do it too, perhaps by discussing how to get started and by giving some tips? Not that any one way is best. Whether reading or orally telling, some people are loud and active, others are quiet and still. Either style can be highly effective. That's why I always feel a bit worried when I hear a staff member saying of someone else at the other end of a corridor, 'Oh, she's brilliant at telling stories.' The remark (often made) always seems to me to imply, 'And I'm not'. What a pity! Joint interest in storytelling and story-reading can be developed across any setting, along with the teaching of techniques such as how to settle children at the beginning of a story session, and sounds and actions that can be introduced to keep them interested during the story. These techniques can also include such important matters as creating a good store of props or how to handle children's interventions during a story as well as ways to encourage them to respond when the story is over.

A STRATEGY FOR STORIES

Developing a strategy for stories across any particular setting needs to be something fully inclusive in which all staff members feel they can play a part, both in describing their own feelings about the activity of delivering stories and in developing new approaches to it. This book offers a variety of ideas for how staff may come together to share current experience as well as decide on ways to improve and extend it. A fresh approach to something so taken for granted as storytime, whether it involves bringing in expertise from outside or employing DIY methods, can be really invigorating. You may well realise that, in your setting, even some of the most basic questions haven't been a matter of joint discussion: questions like when best in the morning or afternoon to have storytime. Is the end of the session such a good idea, when parents are lining up and champing at the bit to pick up their children? Is it necessarily a good idea to have the children sit wherever they want? Do stories figure much in your setting at times other than storytime?

Reaching out beyond the setting is a vital aspect in the development of an effective story strategy. And, frankly, an effective story strategy is a critical part of any child's early education. How any particular child will respond has, of course, much to do with their parents or carers. Living in a home where there are no books will have a big and largely negative impact on their general education. It will diminish the child's capacity for absorbing language and new ideas, let alone diminish her or his abilities in regard to learning to read. If a child lives in a home where no one ever tells ordinary family stories – about what happened last week, or last summer, or what Grandma did when her neighbour kicked her cat, that child is not going to grow up knowing much about family background or, indeed, the incidents of her or his own early childhood experience. Feelings a child has experienced will of course be stored inside. But the currency of talk that may help to make sense of those feelings will not be there.

As Malorie Blackman, the children's author, once said in a talk, 'Story is the best medium to educate children' (Blackman 2012). I very much hope this book can demonstrate how and why this is so. Most of all, I hope it can impart both the seriousness of why we should be involved in delivering stories to children and the sheer fun and enjoyment of doing it.

2

VARIETIES OF STORY

'When an old person dies', according to the old African saying, 'it is as if a whole library goes up in flames'. The saying stirs the imagination: the library represented by an old person could contain all kinds of stories – stories of what life was like 'in the old days', tales about things that had happened during the old person's life, anecdotes about special people he or she had known, places he or she had visited or strange events. But that's not all. The same old person might also have known tales of quite a different sort – folk tales and fairy tales, children's rhymes and chants, stories in the form of ballads and songs. The possibilities are huge and, in a similar way, this is true of us all, whatever our age. Even young children have stories to tell. Their stories may not consist of many words. They may lack in beginnings, middles and ends. Yet often there is a world of story in what they can say. I'll certainly not forget the little boy who came across to where I was sitting as his class moved out of the room after a storytelling session. Pets had been one of our themes and, with a most serious expression on his face, this little boy leaned towards me and said, 'My rabbit died.'

WORKING WITH PERSONAL STORIES

All of us who work with children start off with a potential library of story inside ourselves. One section of that library consists of personal stories from our lives. These may include stories about all kinds of things – troubles we got into as children, things that happened when we went away on holiday, surprises we've been given, times we felt a bit scared, pets we've loved, the children in our own families. You name the theme, we can all probably come up with a story to suit. So as you start thinking about your use of stories, it's worthwhile taking a moment to consider these personal stories as a real resource.

A good reason for adults working with children to make use of their own personal stories is that they feel confident with them. They know the stories inside out – after all, they're things that happened to them – and, as long as no one else is nearby who might have been there at the time and may have a different view of the incident, they cannot be corrected. So as the teller of the tale, they have the confidence that they cannot go wrong. But equally important is how children respond to such stories.

Children love hearing about you as a person. It makes you real. It makes you feel human, someone with a life and with feelings. They are intrigued. So you don't live in the big cupboard at the back of the nursery? You have parents, you have a baby? You go home? There's an endless fascination to such ideas and fascination is a quality which creates engagement. For children have their own lives too. They may be young, they may not yet have very much language with which to describe their experiences. But for children, as for adults, memories are triggered by hearing about what has happened to other people. These memories are important in themselves. They are also what can enable children to compare their own life experiences to all kinds of stories they might hear. Once, telling *Mrs Wiggle and Mrs Waggle* – it's an action chant I'll come to later – I'd reached the point where Mrs Wiggle had knocked on Mrs Waggle's door and got no answer. She'd knocked a second time. Still no answer. She'd called through the letter-box. No response. Where could she be? A little girl volunteered, 'Perhaps she's gone to Costco.'

Now, at that time I'd actually never heard of Costco shops. To my mind – though I didn't say so – I thought this little girl had made a mistake and was referring to Tesco. Quite a bit later, I realised how wrong I was. Costco exists. The child had been drawing accurately on her own experience and putting it into the story. Other children at the time had contributed equally valid but less specific ideas: 'She's in the garden,' 'She's in the bath,' 'She's asleep.' The words may be few. But all were worth being heard and descriptive of life as it's lived.

LINKING WITH PARENTS

The venue was a South London nursery school where I'd been to tell stories on many occasions. This was an evening talk for parents and a large number of them attended. Among them was a young couple with a little boy in a pushchair, and afterwards they came up to me full of smiles and enthusiasm. They said they'd learned a lot from the talk. 'We never thought of telling our son a story,' they said, making it clear they didn't just mean fairy stories or folk tales. They also hadn't told him any family stories or tales about themselves. 'From now on,' they said, 'we are going to do that.'

MAKING UP NEW STORIES

Personal tales are just one section in the enormous library of story on which any of us can draw when thinking about early years children. Another consists of stories that have never previously existed, namely the stories we might make up on the spot. I guess this section of the story library is often less frequented than others. I once asked a group of primary teachers, 'What sort of stories do you normally work with?' Eight replied that they used traditional tales, they never made up a story themselves. The ninth said, for her, it was the other way round. She only ever told stories she made up on the spot.

Making up stories can sound like an alarming challenge if you have no experience of it. There are obvious worries. Even if you get a story started, what happens if you run out of ideas along the way? Or if you can't think how to bring the story to a conclusion? A useful way to tackle such challenges is to consider some simple story structures that might act as the basis for your story. What follows is the simplest possible format. Let's decide that the story is going to be about X. So in this story X will go out, have some kind of adventure and come home. End of story. Now perhaps you can imagine ways to elaborate this most simple of structures.

Who is X? Boy, girl, puppy dog, clown?

Does X have a name? Stanley, Pippa, Ulysses, Bobo?

What kind of character is X? Lonely, inquisitive, friendly, funny?

Has X got some kind of problem or need? To find a friend? Have an adventure? Track down something to eat? Make a sad person laugh?

Can your story now gain its own special momentum as you see X discovering a resolution? Encountering someone who becomes a friend? Arriving at a long, sandy beach and finding a magic shell? Playing football with some children, then being given a treat? Doing a whole lot of somersaults concluding with a back-flip and a very deep bow?

Whatever the choice of event on the way, X's journey in this kind of structure must always conclude with the return home and a feeling of satisfaction.

With such a basic structure in place in your mind, ways of making your story longer and richer may now begin occurring to you.

What about the outward journey? Perhaps the path of the journey could present a series of obstacles? A high hill? A slippery slope? A muddy pond? A river that must be crossed?

Perhaps X could meet an undesirable character before finding the one who becomes the friend? A boy-eating giant? An unkind fairy? A monster dog? A witch who hates laughing?

Perhaps X could get rescued from the undesirable character by the one who becomes the friend and perhaps the character who becomes the friend gives X something special to take home as a memento? A friendship stone? A special shell that produces new adventures? A bone that can create more treats? A new red nose?

PROMPTING CHILDREN'S IDEAS

Part of the fun when you're making up a story for or with a group of children is to hear what ideas they come up with. Saying what they think gives them a sense of ownership of what's being created. They also benefit from hearing what the other children are saying. It's a sharing of ideas (and hence of language). But it's worth remembering that you don't necessarily have to go along with everything anyone says. Ideas can be aired but not necessarily pursued. 'A monster? *Oooh!* Wouldn't that be frightening!' 'And what was that other thing I heard? A big, bad wolf, did you say? *Woooh*, we better run!' Using this sort of approach, acknowledging what is said but not necessarily pursuing it, you can stick with the structure you'd had in your mind but vary the details when a child suggests something more appealing than what you'd thought of. So maybe you'd planned to make your story end with a beach. Instead, someone suggests a funfair. Well, why not? X could have a go on the big wheel, then eat an ice-cream and decide to go home. Why not?

Useful practice for making things up can be obtained through trying out some simple questions when you're telling a familiar nursery rhyme, chant or folk tale. Drawing on ideas from your audience consists not only of asking questions but being open to the answers given. Consider, for instance, the well-known nursery rhyme that describes Doctor Foster going to Gloucester in a shower of rain (see Appendix 1). We all know that, on this journey, Doctor Foster had an unfortunate accident. He fell in a puddle right up to his middle. We also know he never went to Gloucester again. But what we can't be sure of – and what can be enormous fun to find out – is whether and how Doctor Foster ever got out of the puddle. Did he perhaps drown in the puddle? Or did some people pull him out? The possibilities are many. Perhaps someone threw him a rope and pulled him out. Or perhaps the puddle was so deep he had to swim. Or perhaps he was obliged to wait till road-workers came and drained the puddle. Opening up a rhyme or a story to children's imaginations not only creates fun for them. It also develops your own capacity to see what ideas are possible and where these ideas can take you.

RECIPE FOR CREATING A STORY

Basic ingredients:

- A main character (a person, a creature or even an object)

- A task (delivering a gift, solving a problem, finding happiness, obtaining something precious)

- Incidents (encountering hardship, finding help, overcoming difficulties)

- Another significant character (a friend or an enemy)

- A resolution (problem solved, happiness secured, quest fulfilled)

For deeper flavours, choose:

- What's your main character like (tall or short, cheery or grumpy, foolish or wise)?

- What's your main character's name (but no name at all can be intriguing)?

- What prompts your character's task (sick mother, inquisitive mind, need for love, desire for riches)?

- What makes your character's encounters thrilling (monster-filled forests, burning hot sun, a demon with sharp steel teeth)?

- Whether the resolution has a wider impact (helping others, saving a species, earning a celebration)?

For special spicing, add:

- A feeling for what drives your character (hunger, loneliness, strong sense of fairness)

- Descriptive detail but not too much (rosy red apple, smiling face, coin that shines like the sun)

- A repetitive pattern (trying and failing at a task again and again and then finally succeeding)

- A repeated question and answer ('Where's the treasure?' 'It's not here.')

- A repeated jingle (jingle-jangle all the way, jingle-jangle every day)

WORKING WITH PICTURE BOOKS

The third great realm of story for exploring with early years children is that of the picture-book story. Many volumes in this section will be ones writers and illustrators have created especially for children in this age range. It's here we'll find such much-loved books as *The Very Hungry Caterpillar* (Carle 1969), and such well-known authors for young children as John Burningham, Quentin Blake, Maurice Sendak, Julia Donaldson and so many others. Here too will be the innumerable published versions of the many well-known and lesser-known folk tales and fairy tales such as *Goldilocks and the Three Bears*, *The Three Billy Goats Gruff*, *The Gingerbread Man* and *Cinderella*. The specific origins of such stories as these may be lost in the mists of time. But it's worth pointing out that they existed long before they got into picture-book form, indeed before ever being written down. Oral storytelling had passed them on.

In my own young childhood, there were virtually no picture books at all. Now the wealth and diversity of them almost beggars belief. Factual books that show, name and perhaps describe such categories of things as animals, fruits, vehicles and places to live are important for the very young age range. But, to my mind, those same very young children also need books which tell simple stories. Rhymed stories can play an important role in giving very young children a sense of the rhythm and sound of words. Then there are the storybooks. Scary, funny, domestic, surprising: it's important when you're working with groups of children not to get stuck on one particular type. Children get hooked on particular characters and authors, and when children are hooked it keeps their engagement alive. But in any one group of children there'll be a diversity of interest and the available choice of stories needs to reflect this.

What an individual child responds to is not necessarily the same as what can gain and sustain the interest of an entire group. In my Lambeth sessions, my practice was to repeat a book with a strong storyline over at least two or three successive story sessions to see how it would go down with my audience. This trial run would help me decide whether to carry on telling it on some further occasions. As I've said before, children love repetition and when a book wins favour with a group, the telling of it can be profitably continued until they know it inside out. It runs counter to how children learn and enjoy not to repeat a good book because you think they'll get bored. On the other hand, a book which does not win early favour is best quietly set aside.

As well as the book with the strong storyline, I'd also introduce one or two other books of a different type and strength – perhaps a rhyming book, a naming book or a book with very few words – to lead up to the particular story on which I'd intend to focus my main effort. But I also discovered that in any book-reading session, it could be extremely effective to introduce stuff that was not in a book at all – perhaps a nursery rhyme or song that matched the story which was my main focus, or perhaps a chant I'd specially created as an introduction to it. By employing such devices, the sense of freedom and creativity of your story session can be heightened and the level of participation increased. Making use of props can also contribute to the children's engagement. Chants, songs, props: all such stuff assists with the feeling that stories are not a chore to be endured. They are – or should be – pure pleasure.

WATCHING OUT FOR PROBLEMS

It's a good test of any picture book to read it to a group of children seated in front of you as opposed to an individual child sitting next to you or on your lap. I'm not sure if the publishers of such books are always aware how demanding this can be. Watch out for picture books where the text is not evenly spread between pages. Even if you've prepared yourself beforehand, it can be a real downer to find yourself turning over a page to one where the space taken up by the words far outbalances the illustrations. Your audience's attention is almost bound to wander, especially if you as the story reader are struggling to get through the words. Reading to a group can also be a problem if an illustrator has put several pictures of the same character onto the same page. With an individual child, you can cope with this. For a group, it confuses their eyes and their understanding. Are there now several monkeys, not just the one? As the story reader you have to become skilled at pointing to the parts of a page which need to be noticed by your audience while sometimes covering up the rest with your arm.

It hardly needs saying that, with any picture-book story, the illustrations form a vital part. When you're choosing picture-book versions of the best-known traditional tales – for numerous versions will exist of them all – be careful to look for one where both the illustrations and the wording are strong. On the other hand, picture books with no words at all do have great potential for arousing interest. What is happening as page follows page? Such books encourage the instinct to surmise. Equally, they can fail completely unless, where necessary, you as the person turning the pages can quietly convey to your audience some sense of what may be going on.

SELECTING STORIES ACROSS
THE AGE RANGE

Now let's get back to the range of stories from which you may select for using with early years children. Obviously there are enormous differences between most two-year-olds and most five-year-olds. But in practice, being overly focused on age is not invariably what is needed. In early years settings where the total number of children is not big enough to warrant separating them into different age groups for storytime, you can often see the younger children also enjoying the more demanding story being offered for the benefit of the older ones. I think this happens because of the way in which the sharing of stories becomes a communal experience. There's something about its directness that proves involving, especially when the stories are being told orally. Besides, many of the storytelling techniques that prove effective with early years children draw them in whatever their age. Perhaps for this reason, I've often felt it's a positive thing for the younger children to be sitting among and alongside the older ones. You see them noticing the older ones' responses and then joining in too.

NEVER TOO YOUNG

The session was taking place in the children's section of a public library. I was hoping none of the adults in the distance would mind as the young children in my group noisily tapped and clapped their way through the chant in my story. Afterwards, a young mother appeared, babe in arms, from behind one of the stacks. What had her baby been doing? Clapping along with the children.

However, the differences between two- and five-year-olds do usually necessitate developing different repertoires of story across the age range. Generally most suitable for two-year-olds are nursery rhymes and simple songs, board books, and short, simple stories of the cumulative type such as *The Gingerbread Man* or *Little Red Hen*. Familiar or unfamiliar, nursery rhymes are quirky things. They attract by the sheer oddness of their content, the attention they draw to the sound of words and their sing-song rhythms. Children love to learn them one by one. But it can also be worth putting together little sequences of them (see Appendix 1), perhaps also adding in rhymes in other languages.

As for the cumulative story, its great advantage is its repetitive nature. The story gets longer and longer but always using the same patterns of words which, as with nursery rhymes, lend themselves to being told in a sing-song style.

FUN WITH NURSERY RHYMES

1. Tell a rhyme (with energy and feeling).

2. Add some actions to your telling.

3. Invite the children to join in, you doing the first line, the children the second, and so on.

4. Tell two rhymes, one after the other.

5. Divide your group so one half chants one rhyme, the other half the next.

6. Get clapping and tapping to the rhythms and add a little chant ('and what shall we do next?') in between rhymes.

7. Invite small groups of children to act out a rhyme of their choice.

8. Mark out a square of the room where the acting out can happen in front of all the children.

9. Invite comments from everyone on the rhymes and the acting.

10. Suggest children make up some stories from their ideas about the rhymes.

ACTION CHANTS

For three- and four-year-olds, action chants are ideal. Like nursery rhymes, with which they share many characteristics, they are often best done orally and from memory. *A Dark, Dark Tale* (see Appendix 1) is an excellent example. Published as a picture book by Ruth Brown, its story of a journey through a dark, dark wood to a dark, dark house can also be highly effective as an oral telling. Besides, oral telling can allow the story to be changed. Likewise, *Going on a Bear Hunt*. Whether read from Michael Rosen's picture book, *We're Going on a Bear Hunt* (1989), or told in its traditional oral version, this story goes happily up and down the ages, delighting older primary-age children too. *Mrs Wiggle and Mrs Waggle* similarly appeals to a wide age range. Although to my knowledge it does not exist in picture-book form, it's really not difficult to get the hang of it (see Appendix 1). Numerous different versions of it on the internet can help get the basic idea into your head along with the hand and thumb actions it uses throughout. In Appendix 1, you'll also find two ridiculously simple action chants, with which the children can join in, that I made up myself as ways to get children thinking about particular themes, in this case the sea and the forest.

Because children enjoy action chants so much and get so much from them, they deserve repeating many times over. The better children know them, the more can be done withthem later in terms of enabling children to retell them, draw them or create their own additional scenarios. It's another of their great values that they can be enormous fun to reinvent. Some parents I once worked with brilliantly re-created *Going on a Bear Hunt* as *Going to See Father Christmas*. *Mrs Wiggle and Mrs Waggle* proves equally engaging as *Mr Wiggle and Mr Waggle* or *Mrs Wishy and Mrs Washy* or, in a clever new version I heard from an early years teacher, as the story of two spacemen called Zig and Zag.

TRADITIONAL TALES AS A
BEDROCK OF REPERTOIRE

By the time children are four or five years old, they should be able to respond to stories with a much wider range of characters and backgrounds. Whether read from picture books or orally told, the well-known traditional tales such as *Goldilocks and the Three Bears* or *Cinderella* provide the bedrock of a suitable repertoire. They also represent a challenge. Such stories owe their survival into the present day to the story collectors of the past, the Grimm Brothers and Charles Perrault among them. By now they've become so familiar to most of us that we can all too easily assume that even young children will already know them. As a result, we can neglect to give them the attention they deserve. When the Lambeth Libraries Storytelling Scheme was originally set up by Janet Hill, her initiative was partly prompted by meeting children on Lambeth council estates who'd never even heard of Cinderella or Goldilocks. It's different now. Disney films, TV and iPads have made so many traditional tales so widely available in animated form that they've become familiar fare. Yet as one storyteller of my acquaintance used to point out, no story starts out as familiar to young children who haven't heard it before. We shouldn't pass over the well-known tales. There are many reasons why they engage children. These range from the situations they portray and the emotional responses they provoke to the rhythmic repetitions which are so often a basic part of their format. Repetition helps children to remember. Remembering helps them join in. Besides, there's nothing like fairy tales and folk tales for bringing about a sense of wonder and fellowship with others. For Marie Shedlock, an early writer on storytelling, perhaps the chief attraction of fairy tales is that they

33

represent the child as 'living in brotherly friendship with nature and all creatures' (Shedlock 1951, p.89; originally published in 1915).

WIDENING THE RANGE

Alongside the well-known fairy tales of Western culture, another equally powerful resource can be found in the folk tales and fairy tales from less familiar cultures that have by now become available to us, many in picture-book form. Some may raise issues which can seem off-putting. Unfamiliar names of people and places? How do you pronounce them? Short of asking around to see if anyone can help (and perhaps there's a parent who could, or even an online site) you generally have to take the risk, try the name out on your own tongue till you feel you've got a pronunciation that sounds convincing, and then go ahead and use it. It's worth it if, in this way, you can engage your audience with the sense of something fascinatingly new.

Take Tiddalick, the thirsty frog in an Aboriginal folk tale who drinks up all the water in the land around, getting fatter and fatter until the other animals hit upon the idea of making him laugh so much he can't help letting out all the water he has consumed. Or Abiyoyo, the enormous and voracious giant who, in a South African story (Seeger 1987), is defeated by a special song sung by the small boy in the story and his guitar-playing father. When Betty Rosen, one of the inspiring figures behind the current revival of storytelling, told the Abiyoyo tale to an early years class (it was her first venture with such young children), she was amazed by their response. The children absolutely loved the story and over the following days and weeks, as she has described them, 'Abiyoyo became a household word in the nursery and joined the folklore of their common culture in a way that no other storybook in use had done up to that point' (Rosen 1991, p.19).

Both the story of Tiddalick and that of Abiyoyo originated as traditional tales of the cultures from which they derive. Both have come into wider knowledge through picture-book tellings. Both stories would make a good resource for early years workers who want to try making the transition from story-reading to oral telling. After all, it was as oral tales that both started off.

The modern availability of stories from such a wide range of cultures – Ethiopia, Somalia, Russia, China, Mexico, India, Japan and so on – has infinitely enlarged our stock of stories for early years children. But stories from such sources don't just enliven our stock. They're also needed for giving young children a beginning sense of the multiple fascinations of the world around us. Tellability is not the only thing that makes a story important. In most of our cities and in some rural parts too, the population is now ethnically very diverse. In consequence, early years groups will often include children from a variety of language backgrounds. I believe it's essential that the menu of stories presented to them should reflect something of that variety. But I also think the same is of value where such a variety of people is not, or not yet, a feature. A multi-ethnic world has a great deal to offer us all. Stories can provide a stepping-stone to an acceptance and understanding of its interest and its value.

PICTURE BOOKS AS A WAY TO MOVE INTO ORAL STORYTELLING

Traditional tales in picture-book form are a great resource for story-reading. But because they also provide an excellent source of material for oral telling, they can be especially helpful to people keen to try making the transition from reading to telling. This is because much of the work of digesting and simplifying the story has, with luck, already been done by the writer who is retelling the tale and also by the illustrator. If the illustrator has done a good job, his or her illustrations will give a convincing sense of the landscape of the story. This of itself will assist the work of visualisation which the oral teller must do as part of the task of absorbing the story sufficiently well to be equipped to tell it. But more of that anon. Meantime, I should mention another advantage of picture books as a source of good stories to tell. While all libraries worth their salt will have numerous collections of old and new folk tales and fairy tales from this country and many others, the job of finding within them a story suitable for early years children can represent a great deal of work. You might eventually come across a little jewel such as the story of *The Tiger and the Mouse* (see Appendix 1). But it could take some time. Picture-book authors who retell traditional stories have done a lot of that kind of research for you.

Stories are so much more than words. They are patterns of experience. They can make sense of what is happening to us. They can provide food for our minds. That's why their vast variety is so important. Like life itself, they are full of surprises and satisfactions, awakening and exciting our taste buds and giving us a fresh appetite for discovering the world around us.

3

PREPARING YOURSELF

Being ready is half the battle. Not that doing stories with children should ever be a battle. But if you're not prepared, it can prove a dreadful experience. An early years organiser once told me why she was employing me to run storytelling training workshops for her outer London borough. On her first day as a nursery nurse, she'd been briskly informed by one of her superiors that she was to do the morning's story session. She was horrified. She didn't yet know the children. She had no idea what books they had in the nursery and didn't have time to look at any to see what was in them. She had no idea how to project herself to the children nor how to deliver a session. In the event, the experience was a total nightmare. She felt dreadfully self-conscious and ineffective. Now, years later, as early years organiser for her borough, she was sure she never wanted anyone else to have that same kind of experience.

To a large extent, the art of presentation can only be developed through practice as, day after day, you get to know your children's likes and dislikes, what excites them and what puts them off and how they relate to each other and you. Over time you build up your knowledge of stories, getting to know what stories are available, how to make them work and how to sense what will suit a particular audience and when they might be at their most receptive. You learn what your voice can do, how important it is to accept the voice you've got, while also becoming aware of how to make the best use of what you've got by speaking as clearly as you can, not rushing your words and employing a variety of tone and volume. Over time, you probably also assemble a collection of props which you can use to interest the children, helping your stories to come across to the best possible advantage. Alongside all that, you might create a repertoire of activities that can engage children in the story you've shared with them after the story session itself. When you're new to the job or have not yet warmed to it, however, you need to prepare yourself for a number of challenges.

CONFRONTING YOUR FEARS

For many adults, one of the most intimidating challenges about doing stories with children is not the children themselves but the prospect of being observed by other adults. I've heard it so many times. 'I'm fine in front of the children. It's the other adults I can't bear.' If you're young, you may feel conscious that everyone else is more experienced than you. Or perhaps you're the sort of person who never likes being watched: you are self-conscious. Maybe you don't much like the sound of your own voice: perhaps you think that you're too quiet or, as one parent once told me of herself, that your voice is too deep. Or maybe English is not your first language: you think other adults will look down on your accent and vocabulary and how you form your sentences. Or you're female and where you grew up, girls were expected to keep quiet in public. Or maybe you're not a confident reader. Or you never heard any stories when you were a child yourself: you don't feel comfortable with them.

The difficulties are legion. Thinking about them is a good first step towards preparing yourself for your story work with children. Staff training and staff discussions can also help. But I'll come to that topic in a later chapter. Here, as part of your preparation, I'd like to suggest some further steps towards developing a more positive attitude.

You feel inexperienced. But it's worth remembering that everyone starts off without experience.

You're not confident about reading or speaking in front of other people. Yet isn't it possible that, if you go through the story you've selected beforehand, becoming aware of what's in it, adapting it where necessary, perhaps even reading it aloud, you'd feel a lot better about it? Besides, stories don't have to sound perfect as though they were on TV.

You become self-conscious when you're doing a story. All of a sudden, you're thinking your voice sounds dreadfully boring and altogether too quiet. And that's when you start shouting. But what if you took a moment to realise that you are the owner of your voice, it's the same one you use all the time and, in fact, you can develop it. In a way, it's like learning to cook or drive or keep fit. And how better to learn about developing your voice than through doing stories?

Perhaps you're not a first-language English speaker. Yet many children are in the same position. Besides, all children benefit from hearing different accents, languages and ways of speaking. If you look into your personal memories, you might even recall a rhyme or story in your own first language that you could share with the children. They'd probably be very intrigued and also enjoy it.

You're female and perhaps feel shy because, as has already been suggested, it may have mostly been men who talked in public in your own growing-up experience. If so, you could take a new sense of empowerment from the changes that make our modern world an arena in which all can speak out regardless of gender.

Finally, and perhaps this is the most important point of all, if every one of us adults hung back, not telling stories to children because of our fears, there'd be no one to do this very good thing of sharing stories with the children around us.

CHOOSING A BOOK TO READ TO YOUR GROUP

Now to move on to the matter of selecting your story. If you're going to be reading rather than telling, and to a group rather than an individual child, it would probably be asking for trouble from the outset to allow children to take a book from the book box or shelf, thrust it at you and demand that you read it whatever it is. You need to be the one to choose what to read and if you're new to reading aloud or generally feel uncertain about it, it may be best not to choose a book that someone else has recently made a favourite with the particular group with which you'll be working. It is better to find a book you yourself really like: apart from anything else, this means you'll already have become familiar with it before you present it to an audience.

A useful part of selecting a book to show and read is to think how it might link to what's going on in your group here and now. The season of the year? Particular things you're all doing like watching tadpoles or growing seeds? New children who have joined the group or new baby brothers or sisters who have been born into the families of your group members? Outings you might all be taking together? Special interests? The possible links are innumerable. But it's always good to remember that, whatever links a book might satisfy, the story it tells will need to be strong enough in itself to hold the interest of your group. If you yourself enjoy it, that makes a very good start.

PREPARING THE BOOK

Preparing the book you've selected means paying attention to more than what's actually on its pages. It means considering what opportunities for development are offered by the words and illustrations. One book I returned to many times was a picture book about three highwaymen robbers. The story was set in the past, the pictures were attractively bold and a desirably happy ending occurred as the three robbers stopped robbing and became reformed characters. A big attraction of the story for me was that its theme offered some wonderful opportunities to bring a bit of drama into the telling, thus making the situations it presented come alive.

For example, scenes where the highwaymen were accosting potential victims seemed to invite me as the story reader to ham it up a bit by speaking roughly and loudly: 'Get your hands up! Get outside! Give us your money! *Hurry up!*' Another opportunity for development presented itself in scenes where the robbers were collecting their loot. Here was a chance to think about what the robbers might be interested in getting. Money, jewellery, posh clothes? Children listening to the story relished the chance to come out with suggestions – earrings, necklaces, bangles, bracelets, watches, ear studs, coins. This in turn gave the entire group the opportunity to hear the words for such items and absorb what could well have been new words for some. 'Come on.

Hand 'em over. Give 'em 'ere!' The story invited impromptu elaboration which didn't need to stop with what different items the highwaymen might have taken. It offered the chance to think about the various jewels with which items might have been studded. 'Ruby, emerald, diamond. Oh yes, that looks very nice. We'll get a lot of money for that.'

EXPANDING OR CHANGING WHAT'S IN THE BOOK

What was true with the three highwaymen story can be applied to a wide variety of situations that form the context of a story. A character may be out at sea or running or walking through a wood. Either could be a situation that's worth exploring. What kinds of things might be seen in a wood? The pictures in whatever book you're preparing should provide you with a good start. Trees, flowers, fallen leaves, brambles, moss, stones, paths, animal tracks, holes in the ground: what the pictures portray can be pointed out in such a way as to help your audience really notice what's there. This in turn develops their ability to use the appropriate words. So even as the story's character is entering the wood – let's say it's Little Red Riding Hood – you as the story reader might look up at your audience and quietly ask, 'I wonder what Little Red Riding Hood might see?'

Becoming aware of where you might expand on a scene can be an important part of your preparation. The first time round with the story, the children may not contribute much. The second or third time round – and repeating stories is something I strongly advocate – you could be both surprised and delighted at how much the children have picked up both in terms of vocabulary and expression. However, this raises some important issues. First, expanding on particular parts of a story is never a good idea if it's going to destroy the story's onward movement. Too much talk can kill a story and create chaos. Second comes an often-asked question: is it actually permissible to change the wording of a picture book you're presenting by adding or removing words or rewording certain phrases? My own answer to this is yes, it is permissible and sometimes essential.

Reading a book to a group of children is not the same as reading to an individual child. It's more demanding. With an individual child, it'll probably be clear to the child when you are actually reading the words as printed or generally talking around them. Any extra things you say would probably be in response to what the child asks or says. It's not wholly different with a group. But with a group, you have to be conscious of trying to make the story work for all the children who are present. Preparing it beforehand will show you where there's too much text on a page and where it may have to be either shortened or simplified if the attention of the group is to be retained. Preparation will also alert you to where wordings may need to be adapted. I don't think any children's author who cares about children would object to such a practice. After all, your objective is to make their book work as well as it possibly can for its audience.

HOLDING THE BOOK

If you're new to the job of story-reading to an audience, another part of your preparation will be to practise how you hold the book. It's not as obvious or easy as people might expect. Ideally, you'll be holding the book in such a way that the children in front of you can clearly see the pictures. The best way to do this is to hold the book open with one of your hands (probably your left hand if you're right-handed).

Grasping the bottom of it leaves your other hand free to turn the pages. Depending on the size of your group and the size of the illustrations, you'll also need to practise swivelling the book from one side of the group to the other so that all eyes get a sight of what's there. There's nothing worse than a chorus of 'Can't see!' from your audience. Sometimes you might also need to give children a closer look at the pictures, if necessary by getting up to move with the book from one side of your group to the other. Particularly with younger children in the early years age range, you'll also need to be ready to point to important features in the pictures, naming them as you go along.

HOW TO BEGIN

After all your preparation, you'll arrive at your first time of reading the book that you've selected to your particular audience. How will you begin? This is also worth thinking about in advance. One approach is to get the children into the mood for a book by telling them why you like it, then showing them the cover and stating the title of the book and the name of the author before you begin. Or you could take a different tack by saying something intriguing about the theme of the book – 'Have you ever looked up at the sky and wondered if it might fall down? Well, here's a story about someone who did that.' Or you might produce a prop – some kind of interesting object or toy – and after saying it's going to be in the story, get started on the story itself. Spend a moment thinking about these different options while doing your preparation and you'll be more ready to try one of them out. You can always choose a different approach next time.

HOW TO PROCEED

If you're an experienced storybook presenter, you'll already have developed some routines in regard to how many books you'll include in any one session and how many times you'll return to any one of them in subsequent sessions. These questions can be addressed in different ways. Sometimes a book really does not go down well, in which case you might well put it aside and choose another for your next session. Yet it's also worth bearing in mind that children can take a while to get used to a story (just as they can take a bit of time adjusting to a new person). Unless the story really flopped – in which case rising noise levels and fidgeting will have told you so! – it can be worth trying again. You may be surprised. My own sense of things is that it's worth focusing on a particular book with a strong storyline and doing it a number of times. Chances are that, just as with children at home, you'll see them enjoying it more and more as they get to know it.

But it's a great idea too to vary your session with a rhyme or a riddle or maybe a poem. Many poems tell a kind of story and children can really relate to this different way of meeting words and ideas.

TELLING NOT READING

Story-reading is one thing, oral storytelling quite another. Many of the same things apply about selecting and developing a story. But there are different challenges. For someone who has never tried it before, the prospect of doing it at all can seem impossibly daunting. An actual book in your hand acts as a kind of prop. It not only gives you something to hold; it gives you the story, the words and the pictures. In comparison, oral storytelling can seem to raise all kinds of challenges to memory, imagination and fluency of language. How would you remember a story if you didn't have the words beside you? What if you began, then dried up in the middle? What if you couldn't find the right words? What if you couldn't remember the end? Fortunately, all such worries can and should be prepared for in advance. Besides, most oral storytellers would probably say that, once you've got over that first nerve-racking occasion, telling a story is quite different from using a book. According to Hilary Minns, who for some years has been the tutor on the Foundation Degree in Early Childhood at Warwick University, students are regularly extremely nervous before their first time of telling a story without a book. Then, as they see the intensity of the response from the children, everything changes.

PREPARING FOR TELLING

Oral storytelling is essentially a question of realising the resources you have within you and drawing on these to tell the story you've chosen as best you can. So let's take a look at one of the situations people most fear about it before going on to consider how you first get the story into your head.

PREPARING AGAINST MEMORY LOSS

Take the commonplace fear that you as the storyteller will freeze somewhere in the middle or at the end of your story. It can happen. It's not the end of the world. The crucial need in such a situation is to give yourself time to think. In this case, you might resort to saying to your audience, 'And I wonder what happened next?' You'd probably get some immediate suggestions – children like thinking about what might happen – and while these are being spoken about, you'll be getting a chance to think back over your story. With luck, this will prompt you to remember what comes next. If not, you might have to resort to referring back to the children's ideas: 'Well, we're going to have to wait till tomorrow to find out which of those ideas really happened. Or maybe, just maybe, it might not have been any of those, it might have been something else.'

Another possible way of dealing with a failure of memory is that, as part of preparing your story, you could have taken the opportunity to draw out what I'll describe as a skeleton of the story's main events. Keep this by your side while you're telling the tale and, if you get into trouble, you've got a resource to help you. Story skeleton by your side, you can cast an informal glance upon it. Or if it's stored in your pocket, you can whip it out and take a look. An alternative is to prepare a set of little cards with each major scene of the story listed or drawn on its own separate card. Then if your mind goes blank, you can pick up your pack of cards, look at your audience and say, 'Now I wonder what's going to happen next. Let's see.' Then flick through the cards as if to remind yourself of what has happened already until you get to the point where your memory faltered.

All these are techniques for dealing with memory loss. But if you like the idea of them, they can also become a regular method which you employ in the course of your telling. For instance, you might have chosen to learn *The Gingerbread Man* so as to tell it without a book. Imagine that, in telling the story, you'd got to the point where the little gingerbread man has started running away from the kitchen. You've remembered that ahead of him he saw… But now, alas, your mind has gone completely vacant as to which animal he saw. 'Ah-ha!' you could possibly say while taking a look at your set of cards. 'And who do you think was lurking there? It was a pig, a very, very hungry pig…'

Making a set of cards for a story can come in useful in another way too. As you move on to preparing a second story for telling, the cards you've made for the first can be stored away, perhaps in a box, against the time when you want to tell it again. All oral storytellers are prone to the problem of not quite remembering every part of a story after some time has elapsed. Story cards ensure you have a ready reference point available for the future. With tales you've learned from another storyteller rather than a book, this can prove an especially valuable resource.

ABSORBING A STORY FOR TELLING

Now we have to address the question of how you begin to absorb a story for oral telling if you've never told one before. Many people labour under the misapprehension that, to tell a story such as a traditional tale, you have to have learned some kind of script. No. To prepare for telling an oral story, you have to absorb the story to the extent that you feel as if you yourself have been in it. This means becoming familiar not only with the story's structure but with every part of what happens along the way. If only we allowed ourselves to try it out, it's probable that most of us would already be able to retell one or another of the best-known traditional tales. Constant reproduction – in films, on TV and in print – has made many such tales so well known that the wherewithal to retell them already lies within our own memory banks. Think, for instance, of *Goldilocks and the Three Bears*. If, right now, you try telling this story to yourself in your mind without referring to a book, the chances are you'll be able to do all of it or most of it. If there are bits you realise you've forgotten, you could easily look out a published version, perhaps in a book, perhaps on the internet, and refresh your memory. Meantime, even from your first attempt, you might see that you already have the bones of the story in your mind. This realisation could help you a lot. It could make you aware of how, with some preliminary thinking, you could safely venture to tell that story out loud.

But what about telling a story that isn't generally well known? In the case of a story picked up from someone else, you're going to have to try to recall the important points of it as the starting point for your own preparation. If you can't do this as a minimum, you're a bit stuck unless you can get in touch with the teller from whom you heard the story in the first place and ask to be reminded of the parts you've forgotten. Or maybe you could find a version on YouTube. In any case, you'll need to move on from how other tellers have told the story because you're going to have to make it feel like your own. This involves thinking it through both in general structure and in detail. One way to achieve this is through boiling down the plot of the story to its bare essentials. This supplies your knowledge of the story's bones. Another is by means of the process called visualisation. This puts the flesh on the bones of the story.

FINDING THE BONES OF THE STORY

Developing a knowledge of the bones of a story is vital. The bones provide the story's structure. They are the skeleton of what happens in it. To help you first to discern them and then to remember them, you can adopt any of several different methods. First, try telling yourself the story in just four or five or six sentences. This will involve cutting out all the details. Or try drawing your story, perhaps as a storyline that travels through its main events or as a kind of picture or series of pictures of your own devising. If you wish, you can label your drawings with headings identifying each of the main events. Or you can create the set of story cards that has already been described.

VISUALISING THE STORY

Visualisation is a key storytelling technique. It means experiencing the story in your inner mind's eye so that you can feel as if you've been present in it. The same technique can apply with stories you've heard from someone else or with stories you've picked up from books or on the internet. The reason it works is that, to tell a story orally, you have to become able to tell it in your own words. You have to feel it is coming from you. But visualisation involves more than just seeing. It requires deployment of all the senses – hearing, touch, smell and taste and also your kinetic sense. This kinetic sense is what enables you to walk round a story in your mind's eye. And in my own case, I find it helps me to actually go for a walk whenever I'm in the process of thinking my way through a story I'm going to tell. Even if I've told it before, perhaps on numerous occasions, bringing it back into my mind is important. Whatever the situation, the regular movement of legs and feet seems to help give the story a fresh sense of dynamism and energy.

LEARNING A STORY FOR ORAL TELLING

1. Pick a story you like (not one you don't enjoy!).

2. If it's from a written source, read it through several times. If heard, ensure you recall it.

3. Tell the story to yourself in your own words.

4. Create your own skeleton drawing or time-line of the main events.

5. Visualise the story's events, characters and locations in your own imagination.

6. Check you remember any important repeated phrases.

7. In the bath or on a walk, think the whole thing through again – out loud if you wish.

8. Decide how you'll begin and end your telling and consider if you'd like a prop or props to help you.

9. Tell the story and retell it again soon after.

10. Note how your story changes somewhat with each new telling.

THE SPECIAL VALUE OF STORYTELLING

Absorbing a story for oral telling does require you to take the time to do it. Such time will come to feel very well spent. It can make you aware that you know things about life and the world around you and that you have within yourself the creative ability to pass these on. For when you really think about a story in such a way as to be able to tell it, you are making it part of yourself. Your communication of it can feel very natural. You're telling it as if you were there. You're conveying your own sense of the events of the story and its characters, why they behaved as they did and what they felt and said.

Compared with reading a story from a book, oral telling can greatly add to the sense of awe and respect with which an audience hears it. The story in a book comes from someone else, namely the author. The story that comes out of your mouth comes from you. The result is an immediacy which is compelling both for the teller and the listener.

What I've said here about preparing stories for oral telling is all too brief. But I hope I've succeeded in identifying and describing some of the special features that distinguish the telling of stories from the reading of them. Fortunately, no one has to make a once-and-for-all choice between the two methods. The richness and variety of stories available to be told with early years children means both approaches have much to offer. When you add in what can be achieved through the telling of your own true tales, I think you'll agree there's plenty to be going on with.

WORKING WITH NURSERY RHYMES

Some additional points do need to be made, however, about the special department of material for early years children represented by rhymes and what I have described as action chants. Here, word-for-word memorising does come into its own. Of course, there are plenty of picture books that present nursery rhymes. They can be great fun to use. They also mean, at the outset at least, that you don't have to memorise the rhymes they present. But they'll be much more fun for all if you do know them by heart. So it's a good idea – and one that will prove useful in the long term too – to make yourself a set of memory-jogging cards, each with the words of a different favourite nursery rhyme. Gradually, you'll find yourself remembering more and more of them. Gradually, too, as children get to know them, you can arrange them in different sequences for doing with the children. From time to time introduce less usual ones such as *Little Miss Myrtle* (see Appendix 1). There's nothing quite like knowing such rhymes by heart. Knowing a rhyme gives you confidence in saying it and having that confidence gives your voice more strength and more rhythm.

WORKING WITH ACTION CHANTS

The same is true with action chants such as *Going on a Bear Hunt* or *Mrs Wiggle and Mrs Waggle*. Their rhythm and pattern are the essence of their success with children and, as with nursery rhymes, knowing them by heart gives you the confidence you need to lead groups of children through them. What makes it worthwhile to spend the necessary preparation time (probably far less than you might imagine beforehand) is that they're generally so loved by children and so quickly picked up by them. It's the same with the repetitive refrains so frequently present in oral stories for children. 'Who's been eating my porridge?' Or 'Run, run as fast as you can, you can't catch me, I'm the gingerbread man.' In all such instances, the storyteller's memory helps the children's memory, and the children's memory jogs the storyteller's memory.

NO WORDS

At a whole-school assembly. I brought out my cloth of rainbow colours and taught everyone this little chant:

Here's a beautiful piece of cloth.
But what can it be for? What can it be for?

Several older children stepped out to demonstrate an idea – a princess' veil, a cloth of invisibility and so on. Then a very small boy came out front and wound my cloth into a pad which he placed on his head. As all could see, he'd made it into a carrying pad of the sort traditionally used in parts of Africa for carrying things on the head. Later I learned that he was a Somali refugee who'd only been in the school a fortnight. He'd used no words to convey what he'd done. Yet he'd told us all a kind of story and, in so doing, had also established his presence in his new school.

Finally, preparation can also involve invention. What about newly creating some kind of action chant or rhyme to precede a story you've decided to read or to tell? Such things can be as simple as a statement and a call for response. Sometimes, as in the case of the two I made up that I've already mentioned – one about the sea, the other about a forest (see Appendix 1) – they prove just as valuable in encouraging participation and imagination as the story you go on to read or to tell. They might even take over your whole session!

WHAT IT'S ALL ABOUT

Story-reading and storytelling with young children is all about bringing things alive, creating a sense of excitement and engagement. Your preparation should be as much about getting yourself into the right frame of mind as about checking over the material you plan to deliver. Coming next is how the process of thinking in some detail about your audience can also help you to get properly prepared.

4

THINKING ABOUT YOUR AUDIENCE

Thinking about your audience is the next important step in preparing yourself for telling or reading a story to children. With a single child on your lap or beside you, sharing stories will inevitably be very informal, a matter of engaging both with the child and the story, answering questions and making comments as the story goes along. The child may suddenly have had enough and rush away. But that's par for the course, part of the informality. With a group, comments can feel very different.

In *Read It to Me Now* (Minns 1990), a book about children learning to read which Hilary Minns based on her experience as a teacher, comment is shown to be an integral part of the process of interaction involved in reading to an individual child. The child points a finger at one of the pictures and says something about it, maybe just one word. He or she suddenly makes a connection with something from his or her own life. Then maybe the child gets distracted by something in the room. The adult responds, acknowledging what has been said, building on it a tiny bit, suggesting some comparison. At every point, there's a kind of interchange going on. All of this is positive. It's part of the child's learning about books and language and his or her relationship to life. The same kind of interaction can and should occur with a group. But now it's on a much bigger scale. It's not just one child interacting: it's many.

THE FEAR OF FAILURE

The prospect of doing stories with a group can feel intimidating for many adults. With an individual child, it's usually an enjoyable, intimate process. But as has already been discussed, the idea of a group for an audience can induce in many adults a fear of chaos, with either too much interaction from the children or not enough that relates to the story. Certainly it's not easy. But an important first step is recognising that response is good. An adult who sits in front of a group of children and demands absolute attention from them – 'Be quiet and sit up straight!' – is never going to feel happy. The process has already ceased to be the hugely productive activity it can and should be. It has already become an imposition.

Whether you're going to be telling or reading, you have to think about your audience both as a group and as a collection of individuals. At one and the same time, you'll be thinking about how to get and keep their attention and how to manage any problems that may arise. Perhaps the group as a whole is a difficult one. Perhaps there are particular children in it who are hard to manage. Other worries may be to do with yourself as a performer. Is your voice strong enough to carry to the back of the group? Will the children like the story or stories you've chosen? Will there be chaos when your storytime finishes? And what about those one or two children who usually manage to be disruptive? Have you the capacity to keep them involved, or will you need to let them have time out of the session with another member of staff? Is any other member of staff going to be present in the room as part of your audience, and if so can you cope with that? Would you rather be there on your own?

KEYS TO PREVENTING CHAOS

Experience can teach you a lot about dealing with a group of children, acknowledging them and interacting with them while not letting them get out of control. Probably the single most important key is to learn how to make your stories sufficiently exciting and involving that, along the way, individual comments can be heard and absorbed without distracting from the main event of the story. Two other approaches can help a lot. First is to realise and remember that children love repetition – and not only within a story. When the group really enjoys a particular story, whether it's being told or read, it's worth repeating it on successive occasions. As the children's enjoyment increases, so will their focus. Meanwhile, choosing a story that has repeated phrases within it both allows and encourages children to join in, thus using their voices in a non-disruptive way (that's just the same as with individual children at home).

THE POWER OF SOUND

The new four-year-old was big for her age and perpetually bumping into things. She also kept screaming. Group policy was that everyone came for stories, children and adults. I wondered how I'd manage the screaming. Suddenly, while reading *Little Red Monkey* by John Astrop (2010) (see Appendix 1), in which a naughty monkey comes up with a sequence of tricks, I thought about my Aunty Mali. She had taught me the sol-fa method and I suddenly found myself singing four descending notes on the sol-fa scale: doh, soh, meh, doh. Except I sang them as la, la, la, la. On the instant, the screaming stopped. The child looked up. 'Quick,' I thought to myself. 'Do it again.' Again she listened. Soon I added some words, sing-song style: 'What shall I do today, I wonder?' It worked. Each new monkey trick, same little riff. That day's experience taught me a lot.

A second approach to avoiding chaos is to develop the children's sense of involvement with the whole business of doing stories. Children love to imitate adults, so if you've been reading a story from a book, why not give the children a bit of quiet time after you've finished when they can sit by themselves with a book that they've chosen and do some of the things they've seen you doing: turning over the pages one by one, looking at the pictures to see what story the pictures tell and, if they're already familiar with the story, retelling it to themselves in their own way? If you've been telling a story rather than reading, why not allow children time to talk about the story as a group after it's over, then maybe retelling it to you or to each other? Of course, you must allow enough time for this to happen. Being in a hurry doesn't help.

WORRIES ABOUT BEING OBSERVED

Another positive approach to dealing with worries about your audience is to try to be upfront about them with yourself. This involves separating any fears you have about other adults who might be part of your audience from your worries about the children themselves. First, let's look again at those worries provoked by the prospect of other adults seeing and hearing what you do. As has already been said, this fear is common to many people who work with children. They feel they're okay with the children but embarrassed to be seen by other adults doing such things as making animal noises. Get used to it. Such worries are far more likely to be to do with yourself than with anyone else. They probably arise from a sense you may have of being judged as if you were an actor on a stage. This can feel extremely intimidating, laying you open to all kinds of criticisms that essentially come from within yourself. Your voice, your posture, your ability to deliver the story: all can come under attack from your internal critic who, sadly, can all too easily be brought out by the presence of other adults (colleagues included), whether or not they're actually part of the group. Sitting in front of you or standing nearby, they can seem to be judging you even as you get going. And to you, they may well seem to be adopting a very superior, mocking tone, regarding you as silly if you make those animal noises or extravagant gestures. Or incompetent if you trip over a word. Or insufficiently educated if you speak in your own voice and accent.

Or you may feel especially vulnerable because, in your own life experience, it's been men who do the talking. But our society today sees women participating equally with men in every aspect of the world of story, including in storytelling. Besides, if every one of us adults hung back, not telling or reading stories to children because of our fears, there'd be no one to do this very good thing of sharing stories with the children around us.

Even more important is to recognise how doing stories with children is essentially not performance. A theatrical team that came into your setting and delivered a story in dramatic form would probably have enormous impact. A visiting storyteller can bring a similar sense of something extraordinary or different. But regularly doing stories with children is not performance in a similar sense. It is essentially sharing. The person doing the stories has chosen a story or a book they love in order to share it with others. This person deserves every respect. And it's what they are giving that is to be appreciated – the story, the atmosphere, the sense of enjoyment and participation.

In practice, too, it is important as a member of staff not to feel that you're on your own. Collaborating with colleagues is vital. For instance, when there's a difficult child in your group, there should also be a special helper who will regularly be with that child in your story sessions. Discussion between you and that special helper is going to be essential. It will provide you with an opportunity to get over any fears you have of adults being part of your audience and it should happen on a continuing basis. It should help you feel more like one of a community than someone who has been landed with a difficult job.

HINTS ON READING ALOUD

1. Choose a picture book you like and will feel comfortable reading aloud.

2. Prepare by reading the book to yourself and noticing how the pictures relate to the text.

3. Think about how the text will sound, perhaps by reading it aloud to yourself.

4. Notice the flow of the text and when you'll need to turn the pages.

5. Note where you may need to shorten the text or simplify wording as you go along.

6. Pay attention to chances to vary your voice (soft or loud, high or low) or add sound effects (e.g. animal noises).

7. Spot particular places to encourage children to join in (e.g. with repetitions or by giving their ideas).

8. Take your time when reading the book with children.

9. Allow extra time at the end for children to come back to earth and say what they'd like to say.

10. Be ready to do the book again – and maybe again.

TREATING CHILDREN AS COLLABORATORS

The most positive approach to thinking about your audience is to focus on the children and how to set a good tone for your story work with them. Whether you're going to be telling or reading, you can return later to thinking about how to maintain their involvement as well as to such other issues as what to do if things get out of hand. For now, let's consider how some general characteristics of early years children should affect how you approach them as their story provider.

Children do not respond well to being shouted at or ordered about. They are best if there's a sense of calm where they know something good is going to happen. So first, think about how you bring your audience together and settle them down. A good way to prepare them for storytime is to pass the word round that it's about to happen and they should get ready to come along and sit down. It's also helpful to be clear where and how they're going to be sitting and, if there's no regular routine for this, to start establishing one.

Children love to be entertained. You are going to aspire to entertain them and a helpful way of letting them know your storytime is going to be enjoyable is to have some kind of chant to bring together any stragglers and give a sense of involvement right from the start. One I've regularly used goes like this: 'It's *storytime*, it's *storytime*. Sh! *Listen!* What's going on?' Originally created with a group of parents, it requires accompanying actions – hands tapping on knees to begin with, then fingers to lips and finally a hand behind your ear. Repeated a number of times at the start of each session, this chant has worked extremely well for me and the children in getting onto what Betty Rosen has described as 'the toddler wavelength' (1991, p.10). But there are many starting chants (ask around). Better still, you and your colleagues can make up one of your own.

Children like to be physical. They don't like sitting still; they'd prefer to be on the go. Your starting chant can provide immediate evidence that they're not going to be required to behave like statues. Stillness and silence might well be part of the story that follows. But where appropriate, such things as stamping feet, clapping hands and making growly noises should also be part of the experience. So with any story or stories you intend to present, it's a good idea to think in advance where activity of body and voice can be included.

Children love interesting things to look at and hold. Soft toys that seem to have expressions, colourful things that bring cheer to a room: all can be provided by you as the person who does storytime. It's in the job description of a children's storyteller or story reader actively to respond to what children love. So right from the start, you should be thinking about what kinds of things will intrigue your audience and give them that sense of enjoying themselves.

Children like being asked to think. That's why they so much enjoy opportunities to offer their own suggestions. Ruth Brown's journey story, *A Dark, Dark Tale* (1983), reaches its end in a dark, dark room in which lies a dark, dark box. And what's in the box when it's opened up? Well, in Ruth Brown's book, it's a little mouse. But if you hold back from saying so and instead ask your audience, you generally get a feast of responses.

Children like to learn and show off what they know. Through questions you ask, you can satisfy both these instincts. So think in advance about what kinds of questions prompt interesting answers that will add to the occasion. 'What colour is Little Red Riding Hood's coat?' does not fit the bill. 'Why do you think she had a red coat?' is better.

Children like to be safe. As the story-giver, you're ideally creating a receptive atmosphere in which stories are there to be enjoyed. All the learning comes out of the enjoyment. So storytime is not an occasion for embarrassing children or causing them alarm. Rather, it's a time when there can be a mutual sense of discovery.

TAKING ACCOUNT OF INDIVIDUAL NEEDS

Of course, not all children are the same. There will be individuals in your group who find storytime difficult because they have special needs such as hearing or speech impairment. It's wise to ensure that a child with speech impairment is sitting in a place where you'll be able to see and hear him or her as clearly as possible. Likewise, as children with hearing impairment will be able to join in with rhythmic sound-making such as clapping and tapping and also with actions you make, it's vital for them to be near enough to see you clearly and sense the vibrations in the sounds you introduce.

There are children who are extremely shy. It's useless to try to compel them to join in. They must take their time, perhaps looking round at other children to get the hang of what's going on until they feel comfortable enough to join in with the sounds and actions others are making. A little smile of encouragement that notices when this finally happens can be really helpful.

RESPONSE AT LAST

He never communicated. Other children would put up their hands, speak out, respond. This boy never did until the first day I read them Michael Foreman's book, *Dinosaurs and All That Rubbish* (1993). Its story is about how our planet got messed up with rubbish and one sound I introduced (with appropriate action!) was 'Pooh!' (fingers to nose each time it was said).

Afterwards this particular boy rushed to where I was sitting, picked up the Michael Foreman book and thrust it into my hands as if to say, 'Read it again!' As I did, he quickly responded. Fingers going to his nose, head tilting back, he exclaimed loudly, 'Pooh!' He did it over and over and I felt an enormous sense of triumph.

After that, he'd always join in. I learned that he was the youngest of six brothers. Whether he'd felt intimidated, I don't know. All I know is he did have a voice and a sense of humour too.

Then there are all those children – increasingly numerous in the view of many early years workers – whose language is impoverished. These are children who may be not spoken with much at home, children who are shouted at, children who don't get much reason to listen and who almost certainly never get told a story or shown a book. If storytelling is 'a crash course in listening' as Dorothy Butler described it in *Babies Need Books* (1980, p.25), these language-deprived children are not likely to feel comfortable with it, certainly not at first. What's to be done with them at storytime?

Language-deprived children may well be among those different sorts of children – including children with plenty of language – who simply don't like being part of a group. Some will clamour for your unadulterated attention and it can be a good idea to invite the neediest of them to come and sit really close to you in storytime, perhaps with a hand on your knee. Others may kick up such a row of crying or protesting that it proves best for them to be taken out of the room until they've calmed down, then brought back in after the expectations have been quietly explained to them. (If this is to be done, it will certainly require another adult to be present with you in the story session.) Perhaps the crying and protesting will happen again after the child has been brought back. Once again, the routine will need to be repeated. And after that? Perhaps that's where you draw a line. The child is now going to miss out on this particular occasion. Perhaps next time will be better. Or perhaps you as the adult doing storytime will spontaneously come up with something – a sound, a song or an action – that catches the child's attention. You can't prepare it all in advance and sometimes something done in desperation proves just what is needed.

SECOND-LANGUAGE LEARNERS

Another special situation concerns the child or children for whom the language you're using is a second language. Two important points can be made about such a situation. First, it is worth recognising the fact that all young children are language learners. Second, for children who are second-language learners, stories can be of particular benefit. Perhaps the main reason for this is that, when stories are being told or read, language is being used in a non-threatening way – not to give instructions, not to challenge, not to rebuke. Compared with many of the other situations the second-language learner will be experiencing, storytime should be positively relaxing.

As I always like to observe, a story is a journey of the emotions as much as of the words and the plot. Even when a young language learner understands very little of the language that's being used, he or she can experience the emotions of the story through the tones of voice in which it's conveyed. The journey of the story gives the experience of having a beginning and an end and something that happens in between. This is satisfying. It's a piece of experience that is bounded.

Just as important is that a language learner who hears a story is hearing language in a particular context. With a picture book, the scenarios of the story are visualised in the illustrations provided. These will establish the story's context. So if the pictures show a journey being made and the words include a repeated phrase such as 'And he walked and he walked and he walked', it becomes clear that the journey and the walking are associated. For language learners hearing an oral story, the repetition of such a phrase in any one telling likewise gives a sense of what is happening. When the story is repeated on other occasions, this proves even more useful:

recognition helps assimilation. More useful still is when the children in the audience are encouraged to join in. When this happens, the language learners are hearing these words not only from the storyteller but from everyone else as well. This can greatly assist their confidence in speaking. First, they don't feel they are sticking out. Second, they're getting repeated chances to hear and practise words and phrases.

A traditional story such as *A House for Me* (see Appendix 1) or an action chant such as *Little Bear and the Long Road* (see Appendix 1) makes ample use of repetition of words and phrases. When actions are introduced to go along with such a story, another dimension is added. You as the story presenter are now providing yet more help to the language learner's imagination and interpretation. Copying any actions you introduce has the advantage that it keeps children involved and engaged. But it also means they're learning. Imagine making appropriate actions for climbing a ladder or sliding down a hill. From the movements you make – and of course you can employ such actions when story-reading too – the meanings of up and down will soon become obvious: they're being reflected in the gestures you're making. When intriguing sounds are also added – perhaps *Uuugh!* for climbing the hill, *Wheeee!* for going down it – your audience is getting a yet more useful and enjoyable opportunity to absorb the meanings of the accompanying words.

SAND IN MY HAIR

To get the children into the mood, I started playing my 'magic music'. 'That's a bird, that is,' one girl called out. 'Perhaps it is,' I replied. 'Perhaps it's outside, perhaps it's calling us out.' 'Yes,' the children responded, turning their faces towards the window.

The fantasy quickly developed. Without moving, I suggested, 'Let's open the window and go with the bird.' As we began flapping our arms like wings, I wondered where the bird was taking us. 'The seaside,' one child responded. On our way, still flapping, we saw houses and fields and then, quite quickly, we came to Brighton. After landing on the sand, I enquired, 'What shall we do?' 'Build a sandcastle,' was the immediate response. So we made a sandcastle, firming the sides, then found something to make a flag for the top. When I next wondered if we might stay the night, general agreement was expressed and when I wondered, 'Where could we stay?' The answer was prompt – 'Inside the sandcastle.'

So we spent our night inside the sandcastle in Brighton and in the morning, as we were waking, one of the children set the seal on our fantasy as she burst out, 'Ugh! I've got sand in my hair!'

TAKING RESPONSES ON BOARD

An important key to thinking about an audience of children is really listening to what the children say in response to what you say and do as the story-giver. And not hastily dismissing what is said is another. So if a child volunteers something you don't quite catch or understand, it's worth asking gently for it to be repeated. As we all know, children can be very shy. Often they have such quiet voices that you still can't hear what they say even when they say it a second time. In this case, it's perfectly possible, if you ask, that other children sitting nearby can help.

While shy and very quiet children pose a special challenge, difficulties can also arise with children who have a better-developed ability with language than others in the group. Knowing lots of words for things and understanding what they convey can be accompanied by an understandable desire to speak out loud and often. This can sometimes be a pain. You certainly don't want any one child to dominate a story session. Offering opportunities for numerous children to speak and be heard will be one way to overcome this problem – and you can vary how you respond according to the kind of thing they have said. So when you look round at your audience and see that lots of different children are desperate to say something, be careful to bring in both the generally uncommunicative child and also the one who is always keenest to speak. Each child's contribution can be acknowledged. Each child's contribution can be appreciated. But from time to time, it can also be a good idea to give the child with advanced use of language the chance to shine, perhaps by coming out front to retell one of your stories.

As adults, we need to be ready to listen. But we also have to be ready to be surprised at what children say and, although we may be taken by surprise, not to reject it out of hand. For when children respond to stories, they usually do so with a directness that is not usual with us adults. They say what they see and what they feel. 'Kill him,' has come up as a frequent response to the question I ask about what to do about the little red monkey in the story of the same name (see Appendix 1). It can be worse: 'Throw a concrete block on his head.' Rather than looking shocked, you could try saying, 'Yes, and then he'd be dead.' Then after a pause, and probably to general assent, you could continue, 'But then we might miss him – and that would be a shame.'

DEVELOPING A SENSE OF ACCEPTANCE

It's worth remembering the depth of feeling children can have. As children listen to a story, it's as if they become part of the story themselves. This means they can feel they are in it – and sometimes in ways that we, as adults, wouldn't normally expect. I know when I was a child, reading or hearing about princesses being rescued from dragons, I'd certainly be the princess. Yet at the same time, I'd definitely also be the prince, owning for myself his daring and determination. Invariably too, as I admired dragons, I'd feel the deep pain of the dragon.

As well as reflecting their own inner thoughts and feelings, children also reflect the attitudes of the people in the family and society where they're growing up. They're not always going to be attitudes you yourself share. Particularly useful for accommodating different kinds of children are stories or story-games where you can invite children to come out in front of the others to participate, perhaps by making an animal noise or showing how a character in a story might behave in a particular situation. Simply coming out in front of the other children can do wonders for a child's confidence. I've frequently been astonished at the eagerness of all kinds of children – shy ones, silent ones, ones with physical disabilities – to venture to do this. It increases their sense of acceptance and, personally, I always make sure to thank and shake hands with any child who accepts such an invitation before they go back to their place. It's a way of reducing the potential gap between you as the storyteller and your audience and members of your audience with each other. It makes your story session into more of a community occasion.

MANAGING CLAMOUR

But beware! Whether you're reading or telling a story, you don't want *too* much input. Spoken input, whether in the form of questions, comments or discussion, can overbalance a session just as much as bad behaviour can. While it's an admirable objective to extend children's imagination and language, neither can happen if so much participation is going on that no one can hear anyone else. So when a child on your left is saying, 'I went to IKEA at the weekend,' and at the same time, a child on your right is saying, 'I've got a rabbit at home,' and yet another person is declaring, 'I know what's going to happen,' it's time to shut down the clamour and get on with the story.

But how? When there's too much clamour to hear yourself think, it's probable that you've already allowed the story to drift. To get it back, you'll first have to achieve some quiet. Maybe look at the child to your left, finger lifted to your mouth: 'Shhh!' Then look at the children sitting ahead of you. 'Shhhh! Can you do that?' Look to the right: 'Shhhh! I wonder what's going to happen next.' Now you must take the story in hand. 'Oh my goodness, there's a wolf! Dear me, he's fallen down the well.' The children's attention should now be back with you and you can continue with your tale.

All storytimes can get out of hand. Too much participation is just one reason. A windy day or the presence of a visitor in the centre or school are notably commonplace other reasons – and nothing to do with the skills of the story reader or teller. They make it essential to realise how important it is for all story-givers to be able to forgive themselves for a storytime that has gone badly wrong or not been as successful as they would have wished. Early years audiences are among the most challenging you can have: this needs to be generally acknowledged. And with early years audiences, it is especially necessary to learn as you go along. Getting familiar with your materials, whether picture books or oral stories, is one side of the learning. The other side is getting familiar with how different children respond both as individuals and as part of a group. Some crucial aspects of this may not be entirely within your personal control, such as the timing of story sessions.

REVIEWING YOUR ROUTINES

If at all possible, make sure to review the issue of timings with colleagues. Story sessions are commonly held at the end of a morning or afternoon. But this is not generally the easiest or most productive time. Parents are probably arriving and possibly chattering within hearing. Children are tired and keen to get home or have food. Also, when storytime comes at the end of a session, no opportunity exists for any related follow-up. So could it be worth you and your colleagues moving storytime to somewhere near the middle? This may go against tradition in your setting. But you could discover that children are far fresher and more responsive at the earlier time. And you can always retain a short sing-song and rhyme time for the end of the session.

Trying out something new feels risky. If you can't manage an earlier time for stories as a daily routine, how about making a special storytime once a week at the more productive time? It can also be worth thinking about separate additional story sessions, for example for the oldest and most responsive children or for second-language learners.

The ideal length of a session also needs consideration. Again, agreement between your team is important. Obviously, the youngest children generally need a shorter time. Yet even with children under one, if each is with her or his mother or another adult, a nursery-rhyme session can happily last for an hour as long as each of the rhymes is followed by five or ten minutes of roll-around time. For older children, real engagement can mean that 40 minutes may not be too long. Thus the length of time a session should last can become like the proverbial piece of string: long enough to satisfy real engagement, not so long as to put children off. Experiment can prove helpful.

A really useful final step in your preparatory thinking about your audience can be to get yourself a notebook and make it your routine to jot down what you've done in regard to stories on any particular day and how it has gone. What's useful about this is not necessarily going back over it – for you may be far too busy ever to refer back to your observations. No, what's useful is that, simply in making your entries, you're thinking about what has happened on any one occasion. Putting enjoyment first is one of the keys to success in doing stories with children. Noticing what happens is the other.

5

PROPS

'Props' is short for properties, a concept very familiar to people in the theatre business. There, it refers to portable items, other than furniture or costumes, used on set in plays or films. Thus, in the theatre, properties or props are all those kinds of things, big or small, that actors may be using on stage and people in the audience will be seeing. And as anyone in the theatre business would probably say, props have a special kind of magic. For a start, they arouse expectations. If there's a rifle on stage when the curtain opens, the audience is immediately going to wonder who is going to use it and why and when. If no one even picks it up as the play goes on, the audience will wonder even more. Perhaps someone yet to arrive will stir everything up? Will it be something horrible that results in a death?

Props can mean something else too. They can refer to anything that helps maintain something or someone in a position. Good examples might be a stick or a beam. Certainly props can be of great assistance to the readers and tellers of stories, and in a wide variety of ways. Whenever you have a selected object – a shell, a pebble, a bean or a bird – that you bring out to show to your listeners either before or during a story, those objects are going to attract attention. Children will eagerly want to know why you've got them and what they're for.

THE RANGE

And what a wide range of objects can act as props. Soft toys are perhaps the most obvious. A soft, furry monkey with long arms and long legs. A wide-mouthed frog that is a glove puppet into which you can put your hand. A long, wriggly snake with a painted pattern down its back. A little bear. A big bear. An African woman in the form of a doll. An action-man figure. A necklace. A sari. A large button that looks like an eye. The list of possibilities is endless without even starting on things that make sounds. An ocean drum. A jar full of beans. A whistle. All these can be props and the most sensible way to assemble what you need is to do so a story at a time. But also think about what props may become a recurring part of your regular story sessions. Stretched out on the floor beside you or draped over the back of your chair, a lovely piece of colourful fabric might be regularly used to set the scene for your sessions. A favourite sound-making instrument might become the norm for alerting children to the start of each session. It can also help them get into the mood and, in itself, bring an amazing response.

WHY USE THEM?

I'll return to how you might acquire your props. First, let's look at why you might want them. One thing is for certain: they will interest and intrigue your audience, thereby prompting ideas and stirring imagination. I once read about a teacher who, when her class had gone home, put an interestingly decorated box somewhere high up in her classroom and left it there until enough children had noticed it and started asking about it: 'Why is that box up there?' 'Is there something in it?' That teacher was working on the premise – and how right she was proved to be – that even before the box was opened a whole process of imagination might begin which would lead to the creation of new stories.

Stories come in many different ways and producing new ideas for them doesn't have to be the accomplished art of the book writer. We can all have a bash at a bit of it in the spirit of seeing where it goes. Hearing what children say in response to a simple question – 'What do you think might be in the box?' – can be a revelation. Children are often imaginative beyond their years. Often, too, they know more than you think. Props can help bring out their ideas, in a number of ways.

HINTS ON USING PROPS

- Select your props with care. One item to introduce a story can be quite enough.

- Put your props in an attractive bag or box. This will intrigue your listeners.

- Show props before starting your story to interest listeners in what's going to follow.

- Keep control of your props by returning them to their container before you begin.

- Show your props again when the story has ended to help listeners to reflect on the story.

- Hand your props around for listeners to feel and see (as long as they're not breakable).

HOW TO PRESENT THEM

Props can help in introducing a story. In this case, the manner in which you produce them is crucial: it can greatly increase children's interest in what is going to happen. Perhaps you'll have put the props you've selected in a bag. Any carrier bag can easily do the trick of holding what you want to show. But if the bag itself is attractive and maybe has other features that attract children's interest, you'll be helping yourself even before you start on your story. A bag closed by a zip will always make children wonder. Why is it closed? What's going to come out of it today? No sooner do they see such a container than they'll be wanting to know what it's for. What's in it? Why have you got that? Now, already, they are eager to hear and keen to see.

But at what point exactly will you open the bag and show the children what you've brought? My preferred method is to use my props to flag up what's going to happen in the story to follow. So I usually get them out and show them before starting on the story itself. Whatever the story – and with me it'll probably be a traditional tale – the children's interest in the props will also start them thinking about what will happen in the story.

Some storytellers prefer a different approach. They like to produce each prop at the point when it becomes relevant in the course of the story. This approach requires you to be able to lay your hands on whichever prop is needed at the exact moment you need it. So rather than fiddling around in a bag, you might need to have your props on the floor beside you or perhaps on a table close at hand. This method can work. But beware. It can also be distracting to have to locate the particular item you need while maintaining concentration on what's happening in the story. Besides, if your props are too accessible, you'll have to watch out for little hands grabbing them and causing distractions.

If you're going to be reading from a book, the first of the approaches I've outlined above is probably the better option. Once the book gets going, you're unlikely to want any distractions from the book itself whereas before it begins, a prop can significantly increase interest in what is to come. It's also worth bearing in mind that a book is its own kind of prop: handling it and showing the pictures both require the management discussed in Chapter 3.

Displaying your props before starting your story needn't mean giving away what's going to happen. You're simply letting your audience in on what the story will hold. For example, in the case of *A House for Me*, the appropriate props would be a worm, a fish, a bird and a key. Having previously put these in a bag or a box (and I keep particular bags for particular stories), you start by bringing out each in turn and holding it up so the children can see it. As you do this, you name it. Worm. Fish. Bird. Key. This will give your audience some clues to understanding the story to come. Because children are often so canny and quick, some in the group will probably start calling out the words for your items before you do: worm, fish, bird, key. This can prove helpful to others. Hearing words without laborious explanation is a great assistance to comprehension.

After showing your stuff – 'So all these things are going to be in my story' – it's best to quickly put your props away as you set out on the journey of the story itself. You can always show them all again when you've finished the story and are, perhaps, talking it over with the children. If you're interested in providing follow-up activities, it's worth pointing out that seeing your props again at the end can give children great enthusiasm for all kinds of ways of retelling the story. For instance, well-chosen props can give them a good start for thinking what things in the story might look like. Therefore it can help their confidence with such things as drawing and labelling scenes.

SOUND-MAKING PROPS

So far, I've mainly spoken about props as if they were all silent, inanimate things. But let's turn now to that other important range of things that make sounds. I have something I call a bull-roarer. I bought it from a seaside stall when on holiday in Tenerife. It consists of a hard cardboard tube beautifully painted with a bright blue background on which snake-like creatures slither around in black paint. The tube is closed at one end and attached to that end is a long metal coil that hangs from it like a tail. When the tube is shaken from side to side, an unexpectedly loud noise erupts as the movement of the coil resonates back up through the tube. The noise at its loudest can represent thunder or a violent rainstorm or the roar of a very fierce creature. It's a terrific way to conjure up a scene or a character in a story.

Props that produce sounds should generally be produced at appropriate points in the course of your story rather than at the beginning. This is because they have the capacity to bring a sense of surprise, arousing the audience's interest and excitement in what's happening already or on the verge of occurring. With different instruments, you can make such different noises – the croaking of frogs, the crack of thunder or the whistling of birds. Some can summon up the sense of a big wind or storm, or the imminent arrival of a dangerous animal or a character such as a giant or witch. In the case of the bull-roarer and other instruments that can produce loud noises, however, there is one big caveat about their use. Some children, autistic children in particular, cannot tolerate loud noise. Staff who work with special needs children or with any group that includes a special needs child will be well aware of this problem in advance and will refrain from causing the consequent upset. But with all groups, especially if there are new children in them, it's important to be on the alert to possible problems and, where necessary, quickly adjust your approach. This warning also applies to the sound effects you may produce yourself. A scream can be very alarming.

INVOLVING THE CHILDREN

So far, I've spoken as if the storyteller is the only person who might be handling the props in a story session. This does not need to be so. Props can involve participation. Let's say you have a story about the seaside and you've drawn together a collection of shells or pebbles. Put these in a bag of an appropriate colour or interesting pattern. Hand the bag round your group, inviting the children to take out one item each. (Warning! Shells should be the sort that don't break and are too big to go into children's mouths. Like any prop, they should only be used with an appropriate age group.) You'll see great fascination on children's faces as they study the shell or pebble they've chosen, turning them over in their hands and showing them to other children around them. Now lay out a blue cloth in front of the children and invite each in turn to come and put the shell or pebble they took on the cloth. Hey presto! You've got a seaside.

Of course, such a technique (and you might similarly use tree leaves or twigs for a forest tale) is not going to be suitable when your audience consists of a large number of children. But it can be especially useful in a group that contains children who are normally reluctant or unable to speak. Those with special physical needs can also benefit hugely from handling items for a story when enough other adults are present to help them. It produces that special kind of reverence and pride that children show when they know they're helping to set a scene, thereby becoming part of what's happening. Everyone gains from the sense of being involved.

USING YOUR BODY AS A PROP

A similar sense of participation can be brought about when using your own body as a prop as in children's finger-rhymes or a story such as *Mrs Wiggle and Mrs Waggle* where hands and thumbs are key to the entire tale. Another such story, popular across the whole early years age range but especially suitable for younger ones, is *Little Bear and the Long Road*. I learned this very useful little tale from the Japanese storyteller/librarian Kyoko Matsuoka, who founded the first children's library in Japan. In fact, there's nothing particularly Japanese about it. Endearing to anyone with a potential love for a small cuddly teddy bear, it uses the storyteller's arm as the basis for what happens, so it's easy to remember. Other plus points are the plentiful opportunities it offers for sounds and actions and also for expanding on and varying its events. What did Little Bear take with him on his journey? Might there have been a boat to take him over the river? A reassuring sense of security can be given (Little Bear can have a mummy who watches out for him as he goes and gives him a big hug on return), and this creates a satisfying balance with the sense of adventure that the journey itself represents.

MAKING RAIN

Fingers and thumbs, hands and feet: a wonderful way of using the human body as a prop – or in this case all the human bodies in your audience – can be brought about when you get your audience engaged in an activity called Making Rain. This isn't hard to set up – it simply involves getting your audience to copy your actions – and, with a little bit of practice, the sense of rain falling that results can become very convincing.

Start off by clicking your fingers and encouraging your audience to follow suit. If they can't click, move on quickly to making small tapping noises on one hand with two or three fingers of the other. Keep encouraging your audience to copy as you move on to full hand-clapping. Then start beating your hands on your knees. Finish by rapping your feet on the floor. The downpour you create in this way can vary greatly in intensity from gentle to violent, accompanied by rough winds or just small breezes. Whichever the sound that emerges it can all feel very real when everyone has come on board. Then, just as you first created the rain, you can make it die down by engaging in the same process in reverse.

SOURCING YOUR PROPS

Props bring an extra sense of magic to storytelling. They can help make a story feel like it's real. So how are you going to find your props? How can you build up enough of a collection to suit a variety of stories? Where are you going to keep them? Such questions about sourcing and storing props are important to consider not only for yourself but as part of any overall strategy your setting might wish to create for storytelling and story-reading. For instance, staff might decide to build up a joint collection. Or, like one primary school staff I worked with some years ago, they might decide to give props a special focus over a particular period. That staff agreed to hold a competition. Who could produce the most effective set of props for a story? After allocating time for choosing their stories and assembling their props, they then observed each other telling their stories during the week of the competition itself. The week ended with a prize for the best. But from what they all said afterwards, the prize was really no more than icing on the cake. The cake was how much they'd all got out of what they'd ventured to do.

People can learn a lot from each other, yet individual creativity is also vital. Nothing is more likely to produce engaging storytelling than someone who puts himself or herself into a story and its preparation. Some people love making things with their hands. Whether sewing or carving or cutting and sticking, creating a set of props by making them yourself can be the best possible fun for those inclined that way and it can be really rewarding. The internet can be a good source of patterns. Alternatively, you might enjoy going on a props hunt – car boot sales and junk shops can yield good stuff. You might also take a look in your own attic if you have one: some of us have got loads of stuff up there and wherever they came from originally, gathering together possible things to use can be very satisfying. Turning items into props, you're giving them a fresh and unexpected use. But – warning! – as I've personally discovered, someone else in your abode (in my case my husband) may sound very mournful when noticing the absence of a particular object you've quietly selected to put among your props. 'Where *is* that candlestick we used to have on the hall table?' How often have I heard such a question followed, of course, by a slightly weary sigh? Well, you may just have to stick with the junk shops and jumble sales.

QUALITY AND VARIETY

Returning to how children respond, it's worth making the point that the quality of the props you produce can also be significant – not that they should be expensive items but that they should look interesting. Maybe a bit old and out of the ordinary helps. A comment that's often been made to me about those I use is that they're 'real'. Almost none are made of plastic (my plastic spider's web is a notable exception). Mostly they're made of wood or cloth or paper or straw and, for that reason, they look in some way authentic. It's completely understandable if this isn't possible for everyone: storytelling has been my business and I've accumulated my store of props over a long period. Yet that 'real' look is something to aim at. So let me take the liberty here of describing some of the props I've collected and frequently used:

- The hand drum with wooden dangly bits at each side that I often describe as its earrings!

- The little orange monkey who frequently sits between me and my audience and listens to John Astrop's picture-book story of *Little Red Monkey* which I long ago developed into an oral telling.

- The glove-puppet frog who is particularly popular because although I don't do especially distinguished animal noises, I'm excellent at frogs (and you have to work to your own abilities).

- The multi-coloured piece of gauzy cloth that can not only decorate a room but quickly become the basis of an imagination game: 'Here's a lovely piece of cloth. But what can it become?' Who knows what answers you'll get? A garden full of flowers? The tail feathers of a beautiful bird? The veil of a princess? A pirate's scarf?

- An ordinary kidney bean (which, because it makes you think about beaniness, can be just as effective a prop for *Jack and the Beanstalk* as an entire bagful).

- And to all these I should add the bags in which I've carried my props, namely the black bag with white spots, the pink bag with black spots and the bag with multi-coloured stripes.

BUT BEWARE!

A word of caution to end. I once visited an early years venue where a whole lot of grandmothers had contributed soft toys they'd knitted or sewn. But, alas, the lovely things they'd created were sitting unused on a high shelf, rarely fetched down and looking a teensy bit sad. The idea was good for getting people involved. What had not been thought through was how the things produced could be properly used.

That example has a wider implication. Props are really only props. What is important is the story they support. When the story is one that's to be read from a book, the book has to be at the centre both for you and your audience, and it's appropriate for you to focus your attention on it. When the story is to be orally told, it's equally important that the story gets the central place. With picture books, the illustrations are the partner of the words. With oral stories, the listener's visualisations are key. So while props can be very helpful, their place is to support the story. They should never overwhelm.

And, by the way, you should always be careful to check that any props you introduce are safe for children to handle.

6

DEALING WITH YOUR AUDIENCE

Some things become natural instinct over time. When a professional storyteller goes into a room where they're going to be telling stories to children, I guarantee almost the first thing they'll do is size up the room, look around to get an idea where the children might be asked to sit, decide which area seems most suitable and, if there's just the one obvious place, whether it contains any noticeable distractions. Place is just one of the several issues to be considered in thinking about how to deal with your audience.

CHOOSING A PLACE

In most early years centres, and in most rooms in those centres, there's probably what has become over time the usual place for story sessions. A good idea is to review it with new eyes. In many establishments I've visited, I've observed that normal practice is to gather children, for registration for instance, into an area that's boxed in – wall at one end, shelves on two sides. A good idea, you might think. It keeps the children together. But when you look at how the children are arranged there, you might notice they're usually sitting with faces towards the wall end of the space, where the teacher's chair is placed. Where there's a lot of children, this can mean that the rows, informal as these may be, are perhaps six deep. This in turn means that the children at the back are very far from the teacher.

For any kind of group storytime, it's better for as many children as possible to be somewhere near the storyteller. Change the placement of the chair in the boxed-in space so that, instead of being at the end of the space, it's halfway along one of the sides and you can obtain a much more amenable situation. Now the same number of children can sit in just two or three longer rows and when the rows are curved, they'll all have a very good chance of being able to see and be seen. Besides, if the person who is telling or reading the stories invites a child to come out front to say or demonstrate something, the child is much more easily able to do that.

A more natural arrangement of people makes for a more effective situation for the story-reading or storytelling. Who would ever choose to have children calling out, 'Can't see!'? When a book is being used, it's essential for children to be easily able to see the pictures. If any kind of props are being brought out, the same is true. And if the story is being told orally, it's really important for the children to be able to see the storyteller's eyes and vice versa.

WHAT THE AUDIENCE CAN SEE

Good sight-lines to the storyteller are not the only criterion when choosing an effective place for stories. Another is to become aware of what else children will be able to see apart from the person reading or telling the stories. Is there a desk beside the storyteller's chair? Has it got on it an untidy muddle of papers? Or perhaps there's a table with a higgledy-piggledy pile of books? Or maybe just next to the storyteller, there's a distracting box of picture books that children can all too easily reach out and grab? Or maybe the sun is pouring through a nearby window onto the faces and eyes of the children? Better to shift position than have the children complaining. All these are important points in considering how to deal with your audience. In setting up the scene for what the children are about to experience, the storyteller must try to see it from the child's point of view. What is distracting? What is attractive? What focuses attention? As someone who has told stories in hundreds of different venues, I've found that one great value of my story bag has been the colourful cloths it contains. An attractive cloth has many uses, not least to quickly cover up that ugly TV or pile of unsorted mess.

WHAT CAN THE CHILDREN HEAR?

I've said it before. Doing stories with children is not a performance in the same sense as getting up on a stage to act or sing or deliver a talk. Yet there are some aspects of doing a story that have to be considered in terms of performance. For the audience to be able to see the person doing the stories is one of them. Being able to hear is another. But it's not just literally hearing the words being spoken that's important. A story can be told or read in a humdrum way with no variety in pace or tone or emotion. Thumbs down to such a performance.

To make a story come across effectively, you have to think about what the children are hearing and how they are reacting. A basic technique is to speak to a point just beyond the back of your group so your voice projects itself. Significant is to keep glancing around your group as your story proceeds and, if and when you notice any children not looking engaged, to vary the tone or volume of your voice and notice the effect this can have. Sound effects can also make a lot of difference.

Of course, children in a group will probably react very differently from a child at home. 'Don't be silly!' can be the immediate response to any unusual variations in your voice from an individual child at home. At which point, you quickly learn that for this child, who most likely knows you very well, the story itself is enough. He or she doesn't want or need that element of performance which different voices or sound effects can bring. At the same time, it has to be acknowledged that gender may make a big difference here. From all I've been told by adults about their memories of being told stories at home, I'd say fathers are often allowed or expected to do what mothers aren't.

WHERE ARE THE OTHER MEMBERS OF STAFF?

Dealing with storytime also involves considering the role to be played by other members of staff. For a start, it does not give a good message if, in full view of the children, members of staff who are not actually doing the storytelling are sitting or standing nearby doing something else. Alas, in primary or secondary schools, this happens all too often. A teacher who sits doing the marking in full view of the children while their class is being told a story does not give a good impression of the value or interest of the story. In early years situations, comparable things can occur. Other members of staff chatting over a quick cup of tea or discussing problems while the story is going on, or even barging into a group to collect a particular child – it happens. And it's a shame. Movement and sound that have nothing to do with the story distract from the children's concentration. Not only does it diminish their actual experience of the stories, it gives a very poor message about the nature and worth of an important time.

As I've said before, involving other adults in storytime is something greatly to be recommended. It has particular value in helping to deal with the many kinds of difficult situations that can arise – a child who can't or won't settle, a child who constantly wanders away and distracts others. It also gives the kind of general support that makes something special of the occasion. Additional adults can help ensure every child can join in, perhaps by putting an arm around a shy or unhappy child or, if there's a child with poorly developed motor abilities, by guiding that child's hands or arms through any movements that come up in the story. A traditional value of storytelling in many cultures across the world has been that it is a community occasion. This has a practical impact when choosing or reviewing the area where the children are to gather for stories. If extra adults are to be present, they need to be able to be comfortable with plenty of room to sit among the children.

POSITIONING YOURSELF

Many professional storytellers prefer to stand rather than sit when they're telling stories. For a start, in crowded rooms or halls, they're more easily seen when they're standing. For some people also, standing feels freer. It makes it easier to move about. With young children, different criteria apply. Much depends on the age of the children and size of the group. Small children can easily feel overwhelmed. It's often best to keep a low profile. But there's really no absolute right or wrong on this point. Just as you may be a softly spoken storyteller rather than a loud-voiced one, so you may be a sitter and not a stander. Besides, even if you are generally a sitter, it's good to feel able to get up at some point of your choice so you can better demonstrate or act out a point.

SETTING OUT YOUR STALL

If you're going to be sitting down – which I guess is most common with early years children – it's good to think about what you choose for sitting on. An armchair? This can give you a kind of authority while still looking comfortable (a bit like being Grandmother). However, when your chair has arms, you're probably not going to be a very demonstrative storyteller. There's simply less freedom for your own arms to move. A chair without arms or a stool may be better. But if the chair or stool is too high, you're going to be quite a lot higher up than the children, who are almost certainly sitting on the floor. In this way, you are asserting an unspoken difference between you and them. A lower chair or smaller stool can bring you into a more equal relationship. I generally choose the lower position. But it really is your choice.

What goes beside you is also a choice. If you've brought along props in a bag, the bag can easily be placed beside you. If you need somewhere to lay them out, a small table beside you will be handy. But beware! Where props are laid out, as I've noted before, small hands can quickly reach out and remove them. Then, minor or major, a scene can ensue. 'Henry's taken the frog.' 'Henry's taken the frog and I want it.' 'Henry won't give me the frog.' Similar problems can arise if you've brought along more than one book. Put down those you're not actually reading at the time and they're highly likely to be seized at some point when you don't want this to happen. A useful technique I hit upon in my Lambeth storytelling days is to sit on any book you're not actually reading at that precise moment. Then when you need it, you can pull it out from under you like the proverbial rabbit from a hat.

GETTING GOING

It sounds a bit contradictory. But at the very moment when you think you're ready to begin your session, it can be a good idea to pause and do a double-check. 'Henry, you don't look happy. What about moving to be nearer me?' What *not* to do at this stage is shout. 'Henry, be quiet. If you don't want to listen, you can move to the back.'

Now, after drawing a breath, it's time to get going. If you're partial to the idea of a chant that acts as a starter to each storytime, now is the time to get on with it. Start by doing it yourself and then repeating it with encouraging looks at the children until pretty much everyone is joining in. Or if you want to get straight into a story via some kind of prop, now is the time to get that prop out. If it's an instrument, play it in such a way that it draws general attention. If it's an object, let the children see it, then say it's going to relate to your story. If you want to gain attention for your story by asking a question, now is the time to ask it. 'You know, I've been thinking. I've been wondering if anyone here has ever seen a frog? I mean a live frog. A live frog hopping about? In the garden or down by the pond?' Or if the atmosphere is already attentive, perhaps you can preface the story you're going to tell by beginning with a small tale from your own personal experience. 'You know, I once had to get a frog out of the kitchen.' Or perhaps you're going to plunge right in. 'I've got a story to tell you and it's a story about a frog.' Now you can hold up your book if the story is to be read or, if it's to be told, you might just start with a traditional beginning (see the next page for a small list of these). Maybe you'd choose the comfortingly familiar starter: 'Once upon a time a long time ago…' Or this unusual saying from Catalonia: 'Once upon a time when birds had teeth, animals could talk and trees sang…'

CONTINUING

Whatever you'd previously planned to do in your session, it's best if your voice and attitude as you move into your story are governed, at least in part, by the mood and atmosphere among your group of children. If you haven't already got their full attention by the time you plunge into your story, you'll almost certainly find yourself struggling a bit to get and keep them involved as the story goes on. Do not despair. This is where the tricks of the storytelling trade have to play their part. A change of voice (loud to soft or soft to loud), an ear-catching sound effect (miaouw or whoosh!) or a quickening in the pace of your voice: all these can serve to bring back children's attention.

In any case, with young children, it's normally a minute-by-minute involvement. An audience of adults generally wants to get to the end of a story, to know how the story turns out. Young children are often not bothered. Sometimes they get so far in a story and then suddenly it seems they've had enough, they don't need to know any more. Sometimes they've got hooked on a particular thing that happened during the story – a noise that was made, a word that was used – and they don't have any apparent desire to go beyond it. That's something we all have to live with. If a child has become engaged along the way, the fact of that engagement must be seen as a plus. Their interest can be further developed as time goes on.

BEGINNINGS AND ENDINGS

Five story beginnings

Once upon a time...

A long, long time ago...

Once upon a time, and be sure it was a long time ago...

A long, long time ago when animals and people could talk to each other...

Once upon a time when the Sun was just born and the Moon was no bigger than a star...

Five story endings

And they all lived happily ever after...

And they all lived happily till the end of their days...

That's it, the story is done...

Snip, snap, snout
My story's told out
And that's the end of it...

So my story is done and so are we
Time for us to go and have a cup of tea...

MANAGING PARTICIPATION

But the main purpose of sharing stories is to catch and keep the children's interest in what goes on in the world of the story. It's to alert their ears, to make connections between what they hear and their own experience of life, to get them thinking about the possibilities of what may happen in the world around us, to see the world's beauties and also its dangers, to get a feeling for its infinite mystery and to help them feel secure with their own perceptions. All that is a very tall order. Yet it's the immediate and ultimate purpose, for instance of the pieces of dialogue we put into stories, the animal sounds and the actions, the questions we ask and the listening to answers. It's also why we seek their participation.

Previous chapters have outlined some of the specific ways in which children's participation in stories can be encouraged. When you're in the middle of things, it's important also to think about managing such involvement. A scary story can involve a scream. Too loud a scream is not a good idea. For some children, it can be very upsetting. Besides, if you scream and the children scream back, it's all too easy to lose them. Too absorbed in screaming, they'll forget all their interest in what happens next in the story.

Audience participation is a delicate thing. How much is too much and how little is insufficient can only ultimately be judged through experience. And even then, you can't always get it right. Yet it's good to be aware of the issue. For what's true of screaming (or monkey noises or giants roaring) can also be true of talking. A question comes up in a story. A child calls out an answer. Other children quickly join in, each calling out what he or she wants to say. Now you have to deploy some method of asserting the general rule: one person speaks at a time. Maybe you'll have a 'hands up' policy. Maybe you can get away with the less formal approach of nodding at the particular child to whom you're now going to listen, then nodding at the next one who by now is even more desperate to speak. If you regularly work with these children, you'll have the advantage of knowing their names. This can help. Yet it's equally possible, with some practice, to manage things simply by directing your gaze and your attention.

Managing children's talk in the course of a story is not only a question of working out how to avoid everyone talking at once. There's also the issue of keeping the story on track. A sensible approach is to have previously made a judgement on where in the story it would be good to have some general talk, be it ideas for solving a problem, thinking about what's going to happen next or thoughts about what a character might be observing. Then when you're actually telling the story, you'll find out for yourself if you're right. You'll be able to tell if you've chosen to stop at a point where the children are bursting with ideas, eager to share their own responses to what's going on in the tale. When enough is enough, the storyteller or story reader has to reclaim the right to be the one who is speaking. Perhaps it's got to be with a sudden exclamation: 'Well, I'll tell you what Little Bear actually saw.' Or perhaps you've got to put your finger to your lips and say, 'Ssh!' in quite a commanding way. Whatever your choice, it has to let your audience know that now is the moment when the story continues.

MANAGING ENDINGS

Endings must also be managed. Is the story you've been telling or reading going to be the only one on this occasion? If so, you'll be wanting to conclude it with a sense of satisfaction that the story has come to its end and we as the audience have been well fed by it. 'And they all lived happily ever after' is one of the many traditional sayings that, over the years and across the world, have brought story sessions to an end, giving that sense of an appropriate conclusion. Another example goes like this: 'They lived happily and so may we. Put on the kettle, we'll have a cup of tea.' Other endings can also convey the sense that it's not only the particular story that's finished, but also the story session. One that I often use – 'Snip, snap, snout, My story's told out, And that's the end of it!' – has the great advantage that if you repeat it (with actions) the children can join in with it too, thus increasing the sense that we've arrived contentedly at our finish. Simpler still can be the deep breath and pronounced pause you may take after the story is finished. This too is a recognition that, for the time the story has taken, our attention has been in it (we hope!) and now we must come back quite literally to where we are sitting.

AND NEXT...

So the story is done. What comes next? Another kind of ending can happen if at the end of your story you invite your audience to think about what they liked best in the session. Is there something they remember? Might they talk about it when they get home? Would they like to tell you right now what it is they might remember? Finally, after some sharing of their ideas on those questions, there's another step that can be taken. Could you ask them if they might tell the story they've heard to someone special at home? Their mother? Their father? Their sister or brother? Their cat? Of course there'll be a bit of laughter about the idea of telling the story they've heard to the cat. But this laughter is itself a way of bringing the session to an end and coming back into the normal world where we might even imagine a cat listening to our story as we give it a stroke.

AND FURTHERMORE...

There's always the possibility, when the story session itself is over, that there could be some related activities for the children to enjoy: playing with some of the soft toys you've brought (who knows whether they might now become characters in the story you told?), drawing or painting some part of the story, retelling the story to each other in pairs... Chapter 7 takes up such ideas.

Meantime, it can be very important and helpful for you as the storyteller to reflect on what went on in the session. Which children responded well, which did not? Might one of those children now be helped to become more part of the group by having some individual story-sharing time with you? Did you spot a particular interest in a particular subject on the part of that child? One you could now involve him or her in some more? And did you notice when and how the responses of the group were keenest, whether they were moved or amused or when they tended to lose interest? At the end of Chapter 4, I suggested keeping some kind of record, however brief, of your storytelling or story-reading experiences. This could be a good place to note this, to remind you. It's important to forgive yourself if things did not go as well as you hoped, and keeping a record can help you improve. It's equally helpful to note when things went well.

It's also important to notice and treasure the times when you see some or all of the children's eyes light up. The great scholar of myth, Joseph Campbell (1988, p.118), made the observation about working with college students that when, as the tutor, you hit on something the student really responds to, 'you can see the eyes open and the complexion change. The life possibility has opened there.' He goes on to say how he always hoped that students would hang on to that. 'They may or may not, but when they do, they have found life right there in the room with them.'

7

AFTER THE STORY

The pleasure most children find in stories is compelling. They respond, they ask questions, they want the same story again, then they want another. 'Oh, please...' But children can only love stories if they're given them with an open and generous heart and a recognition that, in a very real sense, stories are food for their growing minds. First comes the story. After it, there can be so much else.

TALKING, DRAWING, PAINTING

The story itself is done. Now comes the opportunity to follow it up with one of the numerous ways a story, whether read or told, can be given over to its audience to explore. Before the children disperse from where they've been sitting, it's a good idea to make a little time for shared talk. However brief, this is an opportunity for children to respond to what they've heard. You might invite such responses by saying something like, 'Wow, that was quite a journey, wasn't it?' Or you might specifically invite some comeback: 'Anyone want to say what they liked best in that story?' Or you could move on to one of the activities you might now suggest for them to do.

Wherever they are – at home, in a nursery room or a classroom – children of any age, including between two and five, can be given the equipment to paint or draw the story they've heard. What they make of it will be their interpretation. I once had a nursery nurse demur: surely the children were too young to paint the story they'd been given. After explaining briefly that we wouldn't be looking for anything like realistic drawings, just whatever the children wanted to paint, I suggested we give it a go. Although there'd been lions in the story I'd told, you wouldn't specifically have known that from what they produced. Yet the power and beauty of lions was there. Their paintings were vibrant with colour and energy.

Some stories fall into a sequence of easily identifiable sections. *A House for Me* has a protagonist who meets a worm, a fish, a bird and a builder with a key. Given a paper folded into an appropriate number of sections – four in this case – children at the upper end of the early years age range will relish the task of drawing the protagonist's journey, picturing in each section who or what has been met on the way. If as the storyteller you've used appropriate props when telling the tale, these will now be of extra help to children with their drawing. They might even want to add words to their pictures: 'Hello!' or 'How are you?' or whatever it is they remember.

APPRECIATING CHANGES

When children get involved in drawing a story, accuracy of memory should not become an issue. If a child makes a change in the story (introducing a different character or a new location), I am not bothered. What they're doing is interpreting what they've seen in their mind's eye and, as the adult who is (surely!) encouraging imagination, you'd do well to notice any little changes they make in an appreciative kind of way. Doing this, you remind them of the story as it was told while noticing what they've made of it. Some children can be quite obsessed with particular characters – robots or superheroes or Pokemon figures – that do not fit into the story world you presented to them. But it's my experience that if you fail to engage with their preoccupations, they'll be less inclined to engage with you. Bang! Bang! Dead! Dead! Some children – and it's usually boys – do want to draw nothing but soldiers and guns. If you notice what they've done, ask them about it and comment – this may at least prevent them becoming alienated from stories and books and language in general.

On the positive side, noticing what children have done can alert you to quite unexpected or hidden capacities in them. An example from my own experience had a profound effect on convincing me of the value of giving children time to digest a story in their own way. The class consisted of four-year-olds. *Mrs Wiggle and Mrs Waggle* was the story I'd told them and after it, I'd introduced an activity I'd previously done only with slightly older children. First I asked if anyone would like to come out front and draw Mrs Wiggle's house on one side of the whiteboard and Mrs Waggle's house on the other. When this activity had been completed – and it gained rapt attention from those watching – I drew in three hills between the two houses and then invited all the children to go off, find their own space on their own or with a partner and make their own similar map of the story, putting in any detail they wanted.

When I went round to see what the children were doing, all were working with great concentration and to wonderfully varying effect. I eventually came to a little boy who was clearly deeply absorbed. In between the two houses on his page, he'd drawn a long line of hills (the precise number of hills rarely matters to children). 'See, it's been snowing,' he explained with pride as he looked up at me, then pointed to the tops of the hills, three of which he'd drawn in green crayon whereas all the others were topped in white. 'You see, on these hills the snow has melted,' he said, 'and on the others it hasn't.'

In all the many times I'd seen drawings of *Mrs Wiggle and Mrs Waggle*, I'd never seen this idea before. I felt full of admiration at the way this small boy had executed his idea so effectively and explained it with such keen precision. How much was added to my appreciation when I later learned from one of the assistants in his classroom that this was a special needs child who never usually responded to stories.

A NEW PERSPECTIVE

On my first visit to a particular nursery school, *Mrs Wiggle and Mrs Waggle* had gone down well. And on a return visit a few weeks later, I got a whole new perspective on the two characters in the story. The class teacher told me that, following my previous visit, one pair of girls had spent a whole week making pictures of Mrs Wiggle and Mrs Waggle pushing a cherry up one of the hills. Yes, a cherry!

SCRIBING THE CHILDREN'S STORIES

If children are not yet of an age when they can write words of their own, another positive way of appreciating their response to a story is to act as the scribe for what they say about paintings and drawings they've made of the story.

This method is commonly used, as is the practice of then putting their paintings together to create a book. What is perhaps less frequently done is to put the finished book in a special place on the room's bookshelves, subsequently bringing it out to be shown and read in storytime. That this can have a great effect was something I learned on an occasion when I went back to a class to which I'd introduced John Astrop's story of *Little Red Monkey*. I'd long since discovered that telling it orally made it even more effective than with the book. Here the telling had obviously gone down well: the book the children had subsequently made of it had become their favourite book, brought out at their request again and again.

CREATING PROPS AND SETS

Deciding to make props for a story from clay, paper or other materials is another activity that acknowledges and draws on children's creativity. After hearing and loving *A House for Me*, one class of children proceeded to get enormous fun from the sand-tray their enterprising teacher set up to hold the wriggly worms she helped them to make. Each wriggly worm had been personalised with a round card face with a different expression. Before long, they'd all acquired names and by now, living in the sand-tray, they'd already had many individual and joint adventures.

Early years staff can make all the difference to what children are able to take on from a story. In one instance where children had heard a story in which the hero travelled through different worlds – the underwater world, a forest and then the sky – their teacher subsequently got them to help in creating spaces to represent these worlds. Each was set up in a different corner of the classroom and a few weeks later, on a return visit, I saw a classroom transformed. Differently coloured cloths had helped create each world and onto these had been pinned all kinds of paper decorations – fishes, flowers and stars. A large paper mermaid had been added to the underwater world. In the space world there was a giant sun. With cushions also piled into these areas, the children were able to spend time inside them in comfort, talking and looking at books and – it is hoped – dreaming.

HOW TO MAKE A WRIGGLY WORM

1. Place the ends of two longish strips of coloured card at right angles to each other, then fold them over each other concertina-style in small squares along their length.

2. Staple or glue the first two squares together to hold them in place. Also staple or glue the last two squares together.

3. Make a round worm-face by cutting a circle out of card (a different colour looks good) and drawing a face on it, making it cheery or miserable as you choose.

4. Then attach to one end of your worm.

DISPLAYING WORDS

Adults can put a lot of donkey-work into such enterprises. But children's delight in helping makes the work extremely worthwhile. Words can also play their part. As I've said before, naming things can play a vital role in helping children build their language. Whether big or small, on pieces of paper or card, words placed around the area where children spend their time help them to notice and absorb. So if there are paper fishes, the word 'fish' can swim somewhere among them, possibly accompanied by 'big fish', 'small fish', 'pink fish', or 'shoal of fish'. What better way to help children towards learning to read and becoming able to express themselves well?

USING MOVEMENT

Physicality is also vital in the learning of language. Why else do we lift toddlers up, pretend to drop them, turn them over, tickle their toes and play finger games such as *This Little Piggy Goes to Market*? All the time, consciously or unconsciously, we are introducing and reinforcing spatial and physical knowledge – up, down, fingers, toes. A little rhyme that can fascinate children over and over again is one about two birds, one called Pete, the other called Repete.

> Pete and Repete sat on a fence.
> Pete flew off.
> Who was left?
> Repete.

Essential to making this little rhyme work are the hand movements (or maybe use two little paper birds) that symbolise the two little birds, first both sitting together, then one of them flying away (or in another version, falling off the fence). As well as engaging children's attention, the movements help them make sense of the words.

Similar things can be done with stories. Here, too, in sessions devoted to movement, we can extend a child's sense of the meaning of words. Give children the chance to be a lion (with or without the roaring) or a fish (on its own or as part of a shoal) and the children will be physically experiencing the words we use to describe things. This can make an enormous contribution to their understanding of the reasons for language and, thus, to their appreciation of stories.

Action chants also offer an opportunity to make a story into a physical experience in which everyone is taking part. Before this can occur – *Going on a Bear Hunt* is a good one for this, as is *A Dark, Dark Tale* – the story will need to have been told or read enough times (and with appropriate participation) to ensure children have become sufficiently familiar with it to enable them to pretend they're taking part for real. Whoever becomes the leader (inevitably, at first, an adult), he or she also needs to feel very sure about the words and the order of the story so as to be able to lead the children with confidence through it. Feigning surprise at each different stage of the journey helps the atmosphere enormously.

ACTING OUT

Acting can also make a story into a physically felt experience. Older children are often keen to do this, perhaps performing their enactmant at a whole-school assembly. But four- and five-year-olds can be equally keen and there's no reason why they can't get a lot out of it too. If it's to be performance on a large scale, such a venture is never going to happen without enterprising adults co-operating in all aspects from devising scripts to organising costumes. It's a lot of hard work. Yet it's worth thinking about possible effects. Other children who see it may feel inspired. Parents invited to come to see it may not only admire what the children are doing but develop a fresh understanding of the value of creative expression.

Well-known traditional tales such as *Goldilocks and the Three Bears* or *Cinderella* are excellent candidates for providing the story for enactment. But you don't need to dramatise an entire story to explore the physicality of it. Children in small groups can be invited to explore particular episodes, either in actions without words or in words as well as actions, before showing the whole group what they've come up with. Somebody trudging through the snow, somebody else making and throwing a snowball – when such physical scenes are enacted, they can give huge pleasure to onlookers as well as the actors. And the pleasure can include a lot of happy laughter.

MORE ABOUT TALK

But now I want to go back to talking. How to bring about an easy fluency of talk among early years children was something I needed to learn a lot about in my early days as a storyteller. In 1987, an important new schools curriculum project, the National Oracy Project, was drawing attention to the importance of talk across all ages in the nation's classrooms. Integral to its focus was the value of listening. One of its results was that what was subsequently commonly known as 'Speaking and Listening' came to prominence in education. Now, with technologies of all kinds reducing the prevalence of oral communication at all ages, most worryingly among young children, I personally feel very strongly that the country could do with a second oracy project. Children who today are fixated on their devices and laptops, even at a very young age, may be learning a great deal. But what they are probably not learning is how to talk with others about what they're learning. And while they're not talking, they're not communicating. As the novelist Jim Crace has forcefully put it, talk is vital in all human society: 'Narrative is not just for novelists. We writers simply formalise between covers what is an essential life skill for all human beings. To have no spoken narrative skill is a form of autism. Spare us the man who cannot tell a tale...' (Crace 2001)

But how much communication is possible between young children? How ambitious can you afford to be? During the National Oracy Project, a marvellous co-ordinator called Diane Cinamon urged me to try to find out by asking three- and four-year-olds to retell each other a simple story I'd told them. To my astonishment, it worked. All I needed to do after telling them my story was to say I was now going to invite them to be the storytellers. First, I'd suggest that each person found a friend to speak to and when they'd done that, I'd briefly explain that they could decide between themselves which of them was going to be the first storyteller and which was going to be the first listener. Then they'd have the chance to swap over.

It's a technique I've used ever since, including with adults. In my experience, it generally proves no harder for early years children than for older people. What it does need is vigilance on the part of members of staff and, preferably, several of these. The adults have to make sure there's no squabbling that isn't quickly resolved: 'Miss, so-and-so doesn't want to talk to me.' Equally problematic is if a child has no one to talk to and is not saying so. Or when some children stick to the task while others quickly move on to something else which isn't part of the agenda. First and foremost, any adult who decides to try out the technique (and at the start this was a very nervous me!) must overcome their fear that only chaos will result and the children will experience nothing of value. What I've seen many times over in early years work is a wholly surprising level of involvement and interest. Talking, listening: young children can do it.

It's not only with traditional-type stories that such an approach can work. It can work with personal stories too. Let's say you've told a story about your cat or your dog. Afterwards, you might have a brief chat with the children about animals in general. Then, in the same way as I've outlined above, you can invite them to get into pairs to tell each other a story about a pet they have at home or, indeed, any other animal they've encountered. It works. Sometimes it leads to something surprising. Remember back in Chapter 2 the little lad who came to me at the end of such a session and said, 'My rabbit died'? Those were the only words he said – 'My rabbit died' – but hearing them, I knew I'd heard a real story and how important it had been to the boy who told it.

HELPING STORIES TO REACH OUT

Stories do not stand still. Whenever you tell a story to children (or adults for that matter), you're giving something that may well get retold in the future. Children in the playground may later be overheard singing a song you've introduced to them or playing out some sequence of words and actions. The story may also go home with them. Many early years workers will have experienced the question from a parent when dropping off or collecting a child: 'Please can you explain? I'm mystified.' Then, of course, the parent goes on to repeat some mangled piece of a phrase that has been a repeated part of a story you've been telling. You elucidate. The parent says, 'Ah!' and goes away happy. In turn, you're happy you've been able to help.

But that doesn't have to be the end of the matter. Such an incident is a clue to the big potential in young children's development that's often not given sufficient attention. The clue, quite simply, is the link with parents. A lot more will be said about this in the next chapter. Here it's enough to make the point again that a story doesn't necessarily stop when the reading or telling of it stops. The whole purpose of introducing activities by which a story can be further explored comes from fully recognising how stories can stay in the mind and ferment there, releasing new words into the mind's word-pond, stimulating new links and connections, prompting new things to be said out loud.

When I'm starting a story session with children, I generally tell them what may seem obvious to adults. I say that when a story comes out of my mouth, it goes into my listeners' ears and minds. Then my listeners have got the story too and later perhaps they can tell it to someone else if they want to. At this point, I usually ask the children if they've got someone at home to whom they can tell a story. A brother, a sister, a mum or a dad? Or maybe a cat? Or a dog? Children nod. They smile. They volunteer responses. 'I've got my mum.' 'I've got a baby.' I follow this up by saying, 'So maybe if I tell you a story, you can tell it to your baby brother or sister. Or your mum. Or your dad. Or your grandma.' I don't necessarily think this will happen. I'm simply trying to encourage an awareness of the potential of story to spread. Also that it's okay to retell a story. Indeed, it's in the nature of a story that it be told and retold.

Then every now and again, I've heard that, yes, a story I've told has indeed been retold to someone at home. A child or a parent volunteers the information, and I feel rewarded. But the deeper purpose in suggesting how stories can spread is to sow the seed of an idea which was, perhaps, more of a reality in the past but which I feel is still much needed. It's to create some conscious sense of the story community that is always around us as human beings. Much of that story community is now to be found on Facebook and Instagram where an incident or photo of an incident from one person's life sparks off responses from others who have experienced something similar. It's a kind of 'true tale' forum.

A similar kind of forum can be created through the tales we tell to young children. Why, you might even get a memorable new story coming into your setting from outside. Such a one was told many years ago now by Jacquie, a mother on one of my Redbridge parents' storytelling courses. Not only did she tell this story to us on the course: becoming a parent storyteller, she subsequently told it to many classes of early years and primary children. Lots of excellent writing and painting was done in response as well as lots of laughing, and if Jacquie ever reads this, I hope she'll forgive me for retelling it here.

Jacquie's husband was a taxi driver. One day in Redbridge, he was called to a house to pick up some trays of cream cakes to take to a party due to happen later that day. On his way, he had just drawn to a halt at some traffic lights on red when a very smart-looking man, obviously in a great hurry, ran across to his cab, opened the passenger door, jumped in and sat down – Plop! – right on top of the cream cakes.

Say no more. A story does not have to be old, sad, serious or long to have a powerful effect. All that's necessary is for it to be recognised as a story worth telling. Of course, any story worth telling can simply be told and left. Or, as I hope this chapter has shown, it can be given the kind of time and attention that makes it even more valuable to those who hear it.

8

CREATING A
STRATEGY FOR STORY

One of the most valuable ways to improve how stories are dealt with in any early years centre is for the adults to have the opportunity to think about themselves and each other. Are there some staff members who love doing stories and are deemed by everyone else to be brilliant at it? Are there others who go pale at the prospect? Might people find ways to support each other? Could there be opportunities for joint discussion and mutual training sessions? Or could your setting invest in some outside training?

And what about the practical arrangements for storytime in your setting? Could this be a good time to review when your storytimes happen and where they take place and how often? A new approach might improve things for all, bringing new life into established routines. So what about also reviewing how many staff members are present, who is expected to do what, and what the general expectations are for what happens when children wander away or don't come for stories at all?

What about the stories that are being presented to your children? Would it be a good idea to refresh your stock of books, perhaps invest in some new ones? Could any local storytellers be of assistance in introducing new stories or new techniques? Have you got good links with your local library (presuming your local library still exists)? And what about taking a look at your stock of props, including your musical instruments?

And what is your current approach towards liaising with parents? Are there parents who might really appreciate the chance to learn the rhymes and stories you're doing with their children? Might there be some who, if encouraged, would like to come and do some storytelling themselves? Could you devise some kind of project to which parents might contribute stories? Is sufficient thought being given to involving dads as well as mums, grandparents as well as parents and carers?

So many aspects to consider, so many questions! Those I've raised here are meant as a prompt for reviewing what goes on at present. They do not have to be a burden. They do not all have to be tackled at once. Approached with openness, however, they stand a good chance of bringing new life to how your centre approaches stories. In doing this, they can greatly increase the pleasure and value of stories for the adults as well as the children.

WORKING TOGETHER AS A TEAM

Creating a shared understanding of how any centre wants to approach its work with stories is obviously a good idea. Perhaps it can begin with finding out how staff members feel about what happens at present. Perhaps through informal discussion groups or by means of a questionnaire, it would be helpful to establish who'd like some help with doing stories, who has previously experienced some training and who would appreciate some more.

On the matter of the stories themselves, it would be helpful to know whether your current stock of books feels right for your staff or whether it's their sense that it could do with refreshing. As for oral storytelling, this could well sound forbidding to some, attractive to others. Would people like to find out more? If some members of staff are keen, would it be a good idea to find out if there's a course that includes it somewhere nearby or, alternatively, if some training could be brought into your own setting or some in-house training provided?

At the very least, it is worth thinking about ways in which staff members can help each other. Some will already have a lot of experience, good or bad. Some will have very little. A lot can be learned from shared discussion of this. It doesn't have to be embarrassing. Just seeing and hearing how different people do things can be a revelation. More than anything, it's a way of openly sharing how colleagues of varied ages and experience go about things. Plus, if your centre is large, it's a way to communicate different approaches to the different ages of children across the different parts of the centre.

SHARING EXPERIENCES OF STORY-READING

Ways to organise such a sharing could include holding a group session where, for instance, each participant brings along a couple of books they've selected, either to describe and explain why they find them especially suitable for reading aloud or to identify problems with them. Dividing into pairs where each person shows and reads a favourite book to the other can also be of great practical value.

TAKING THINGS FURTHER

To take things further, you could perhaps share a *Laughter is Liberating* session where, essentially, you're all permitted to feel a bit daft. Here are a few ideas for going about it.

Sitting in a circle, have each person in turn contribute one of those animal noises which are so useful when sharing picture books with children. Dog, cat, parrot, cow, lion, pig, hyena, mouse: make it more fun by having the whole group repeat each person's noise. (This should make everyone a bit bolder and more relaxed.) Then when you've gone round the circle, start again and do some more. Miserable dog, annoying cat, talkative parrot, moaning cow, pig with piglet, voluble hyena, impatient mouse...

Or get everyone to bring along a soft toy that goes with a story (preferably in a bag or box to make it a surprise when it comes out). Then, in pairs, have everyone get out the toy they've brought and make it talk to the one that's been brought by their partner. The conversation can be quite simple. Each person can talk as if the toy they've brought has come alive, perhaps describing where it's been today, how it's been feeling and where it's going.

Or explore actions that might be made when telling a story through playing a game where one person in the circle says his or her name and then makes a simple action or gesture at the same time saying what they are doing such as: 'I am Mary and I am yawning.' The rest of the group then repeats what has been said and done before proceeding to the next person in the circle who follows the pattern that has now been set up. So the game continues to build, each time returning to the beginning: 'I am Mary and I am yawning. I am Giovanni and I am hopping. I am Farah and I am sleeping...'

Of course, these particular games are only suggestions. The main aim and object of any workshop group is to encourage and release creativity in whatever way this can best happen. So your group might prefer to explore what different games the members of the group already know or can invent. It's the liberation of the skills and humour within the group that I've always found to be most helpful for making stories enjoyable and fun for children. What comes naturally for most people when they're with children in private needs to come out just as strongly, and with even more variety, with the children you work with.

SHARING APPROACHES TO ORAL STORYTELLING

Several of the suggestions described above should also prove helpful for people keen to develop and extend storytelling without the book. Whether they are beginners or already experienced, many of the important techniques of oral storytelling can also be shared. One is how to remember a story. Another is how to find the words in which to tell it. Both have been dealt with earlier in this book in the context of individuals thinking about such matters on their own. Now it's time to consider how people working together can provide mutual help with the processes involved.

Let's say that in a workshop group, everyone tries sharing their memory of *Goldilocks and the Three Bears*. They might make a start by trying to recall how the story begins. What's interesting is how many different ideas can emerge about this one apparently simple point. Some might think the story should start with Goldilocks, others with the bears. In realising this, the group has already discovered something important about oral telling. You have to make your own decision about where a story begins.

Say the group decides, for the sake of argument, to start with Goldilocks. Everyone can now volunteer ideas of what to say about her. Again there'll probably be different ideas. Hair in plaits or long, loose hair? A mischievous girl or just innocently curious? Running through the woods for a purpose or just out for a casual walk?

I think you'll find two things will now be discovered. First, as participants proceed, they'll realise they already know this story pretty well (and if they've forgotten bits, other people or books can remind them). Second, however well known the story, people have different recollections of it depending on which version they've read or heard and also on how their own memory works. This point is at the essence of oral storytelling: it does not depend on a script. It depends on knowing the plot of a story inside your own mind and knowing it sufficiently well to be able to tell it to others. How you do this involves visualisation, the activity I've previously discussed as one to be practised on an individual basis.

But it can also be helpful – and revelatory too – when visualisation is explored in a group. Taking the Goldilocks story as an example once more, a group might decide on one particular scene to be explored in more detail by all. Or if people prefer, they can each choose a scene for themselves. Whichever it is – and it's helpful if one person acts as a facilitator – everyone now closes their eyes for the one or two minutes that is agreed as the length of time allowed. With eyes closed, everyone takes a look at what they are seeing in their mind's eye. After the allotted time (an alarm can be set if necessary), participants open their eyes and, either in the whole group or in pairs, report on what they experienced.

Sharing visualisations gives all storytellers (and story readers too) a better idea of the scope of what the human brain can come up with. It also gives everyone practice in putting their ideas into words, helping to develop their ability to put their personal observations into language.

TEAMWORK IN DELIVERING STORIES

Working together need not be confined to group training sessions. It can also happen in actual storytime sessions with the children. Teaming up with another staff member can bring fresh life to what goes on. Especially helpful for shyer or less experienced members of staff can be sharing the reading or telling, with one person acting as the main teller while the other becomes the person who, for example, introduces the props or, like a cheerleader for the children, leads the sound-making and actions. (And, by the way, having a kind of cheerleader is a known storytelling technique in some cultures.)

Or maybe there are sections of dialogue in the story where both people in the pair can take part, pretending to be different characters.

Or maybe when it's time for a new rhyme or story to be introduced, the two members of this little team can, with some pre-planning, swap their usual roles so that now the less experienced person gets the chance to lead the story knowing support is at hand.

WORKING TOGETHER ACROSS
A WHOLE UNIT

In Chapter 5, I described how the staff of a primary school I worked with decided to have a special story week where each of them would visit a class they didn't normally work with and tell a new story for which they'd specially assembled a set of props. Story weeks are just one way of creating a new emphasis on stories and, in the process, bringing a whole staff together. A special project could be created which would centre on a particular author or set of stories. Or there could be a project that involved linking older children in a school with early years classes, for instance with Year 5 or Year 6 children selecting or creating stories to tell to the younger ones. (Warning: this isn't always easy for the children concerned, but it can provide a good learning experience.) Or a project could be designed to bring a new focus to oral storytelling rather than books.

Whatever its focus, any project that centres on stories can generate a lot of communication across an early years centre. At the same time, it can attract corresponding interest from outside. So what about celebrating your new approach by holding some kind of special event? A story week which includes a visit from a professional storyteller, or a storytelling librarian, or a children's author, or an illustrator? Or a story week which makes a special effort to involve parents?

LOOKING OUTWARDS

It's an age-old fact that stories have travelled across continents and great distances of time. But what about stories travelling from parents to children or children to parents? As I've previously suggested, when a child is very young it's often not easy for a mother or father to fully grasp what that child has been hearing in nursery. The child may come home with a few words, a snatch of a tune or a funny little noise that goes with some kind of a name that is hard to decipher. But how is the parent to find out what lies behind these small recollections? I've often been told about parents coming into a nursery or school and saying something like this: 'He's been going on about a naughty monkey. What's it all about?'

What an opportunity! When such a thing happens, or even before, it's time to start thinking afresh about how your setting communicates with the parents of the children to whom you deliver stories and rhymes. How to go about this is a question greatly compounded by the demands of work. Many young parents don't have the time or opportunity to go into nursery during the day. But it's also a fact that many of today's parents do not recall any stories or rhymes from their own childhood. Perhaps they were never told any. Perhaps what they did learn has been swamped out by all the subsequent business of life. There's no shame in this. Yet it's frustrating. If you don't know nursery rhymes or songs, you cannot share them with your children.

One good idea I picked up on a visit to a large South London nursery centre involved a cardboard pocket containing leaflets on the corridor side of the door leading into each of the rooms. 'Please take one' said the label on the pockets. A closer look revealed that on each leaflet were the printed-out words of whichever new nursery rhyme the children in that room were learning in the course of that week. Below, too, were suggestions about where and when to tell such rhymes. In the car, in IKEA, in bed? Such suggestions conveyed the double truth that rhymes help learning and learning them is fun.

So far as stories are concerned, it has by now become common practice for early years centres of all kinds to enable children to take storybooks home, probably in a plastic folder and sometimes with a little accompanying toy appropriate to the book concerned. This is an obvious way to help parents become familiar with the vast wealth of children's picture books now available. Even more important, it's a good way to remind parents that reading to children is invaluable, not only because of the story itself but also because of the relationship it builds. Worrying about the over-dominance of electronic devices today, the TV presenter Jon Snow (2016) put it like this: 'We need to go back to basics, reading to children at night, because it's an invaluable bonding experience and gives them a thirst for learning.'

A MOTHER'S PLIGHT

A busy young mother came into the nursery to find out more about what had been going on. For several days, her son had been insisting on her doing the storytime chant with him – but she couldn't quite get the hang of it. Also, he'd been going on and on about a naughty little monkey and she wanted to know full details. I realised how frustrating it must have been both for her and for him that, not knowing either the chant or the story, she hadn't been able to participate.

WORKING WITH PARENTS

Libraries have traditionally been known as places where parents and children can go together for storytime sessions, coming away with rhymes, poems and stories they've heard either from one of the librarians or a visiting storyteller. In a situation – as now! – when so many local libraries are closing, it's worth considering what early years centres can do to replace that valuable service. One simple idea is to hold a storytelling session for the parents where they can experience some of the rhymes and stories their children are hearing at nursery. A brilliant thing would be to organise such sessions on a regular basis. But even one a term could make a big difference as it also provides an opportunity to have a bit of a chat about the stories and how to talk with the children about them.

Sharing stories and rhymes is one thing. Sharing worries about how to do them is another. Working with parents has taught me a lot about the many uncertainties they can harbour. Is it okay to alter the text slightly as you go along, perhaps leaving out too-difficult words? How do you make your voice sound interesting? What if you cannot read very well?

So what about your early years centre putting on a talk about stories? It doesn't have to be lengthy, it doesn't need to be erudite. It can work by example with whoever is doing the talk recounting a simple folk tale currently being told at the centre, then talking about some of the children's reactions and why these are important. It can also include the speaker retelling some of their favourite personal stories, for example of their own childhood. Times they got into trouble, times when they fell out with friends, holidays they'll never forget – such things can be utterly fascinating to children and it's important to remind or inform busy parents that time taken to share such things is time that creates memories and makes life more fun. Too often these days – it's the exam culture! – parents think that learning to read and write are what's important in life. They simply don't realise how vital stories are in developing children's language, let alone their imagination and social awareness.

It's important, too, to highlight the fact that stories aren't only things from the past. New stories are forever being created wherever there are people. Very often, the recipients are young children and very often the storymakers are fathers. A godson of mine wrote to me that his very small daughter 'gets stories made up by my hands and my brain, but the hands talk like puppets…skin puppets.' That this snippet of information came to me from a godson (namely a male) was no surprise. Ask any group of people about stories in their childhood and you'll more than likely discover that some had a parent who used to make up stories with them. And – surprise, surprise? – that person will almost always have been their dad.

Perhaps this is because, in the past at least, men were generally the people with jobs outside the home. Maybe creating stories was their way of bringing home their knowledge of an outside world. (A nursery nurse once told me how her dad, who was a miner, used to tell her stories about the mouse who accompanied him everywhere below ground. The mouse had his own little lunch box and his own Davey lamp and, of course, had many adventures.) Or could it be because dads are especially good at being performers, monkeying about with physical fun and humour to suit? Whatever the reason, recognising dads as storytellers and storymakers seems to me to be something well worth doing. But wouldn't it also be a good idea to encourage mums who may be new to this to try making up stories too?

BRINGING STORIES INTO YOUR SETTING

And what about bringing in stories from outside? At one centre I became involved with, busy parents were assisted to contribute stories to the centre by recording a simple story of their own. It could be any kind of story, a story from their own life or a folk tale. Then a look-alike phone box with headphones and play-back equipment was installed in a prominent place at the centre as a kind of listening post where parents or children could listen to the items that had been recorded. In the particular instance where this occurred, a wide ethnic diversity among the parents made the venture of special interest.

Another way of refreshing a centre's stock of stories is to bring in a working storyteller for a day or part of a day or for a more extended project. This can help with any campaign that you're creating to extend awareness of story. A storyteller's visit can also mean a lot to children. I remember a little boy in a school I'd visited several times before. Speaking in a confidential and very pleased tone, what he said was this: 'When we were waiting to come in, I thought it would be you.' Clearly this little boy, when told he'd be seeing 'a storyteller', had remembered one of my previous visits. His remark told me a lot about the difference an outside visitor can make – how it can enable children to see how the storytime they experience as a daily or weekly routine links up with a wider world of story.

HOW STORIES REACH OUT

At a storytelling event in Ilford on the east side of London, a young Asian woman came to talk to me. She told me how the *Little Red Monkey* story had become so much loved by her family that it had become 'their' story, retold at all family celebrations. When I enquired how they'd come to know it, she said a cousin who lived in South West London had learned it at one of my Tooting workshops. That's how stories can move – far, far beyond those who tell them or those who first created them.

THE WIDER IMPACT

Much potential can be lost across a wide educational front by a lack of awareness of just how many things story-reading and storytelling can offer. For a start, there's the folk tales. We now live in a multi-ethnic, multicultural world. What a lot the sharing of its riches can offer! And what a lot we're missing out on if we fail to find ways to value and share it. Over several years of running storytelling courses for Asian women as part of a scheme to introduce them to childcare work, I was startled to learn that although all those who attended already knew stories from their own childhood, and some a very great number, none had told them to their own children. Their explanation was the one I've mentioned before – that in this country, it's reading and writing that are seen as being important. But soon they began to realise how reading and writing can be greatly encouraged when children get immersed in stories, especially when they're told 'by word of mouth'.

A similar thing occurred in the storytelling courses I ran for parents in Redbridge. It regularly became apparent among those who attended that they significantly lacked confidence in their personal ability to inspire their own children. Many felt they'd failed in their own education and by now they didn't think they had any memory or imagination worth speaking about. Besides, they felt they had no time for such things. At the same time, they were worried about their children getting on well in school, they were worried about the TV going on as soon as their children came home from school and they were worried that they had too little influence on them. The storytelling courses had a profound impact. As children became intrigued – 'Mummy, why are you going on that storytelling course?' – parents felt they gained from them a new kind of respect.

These small examples from working with parents speak of a wider worry in our society about how to deal with children in such a way as to give them a real sense of purpose and creativity. Giving them stories is an age-old answer that stares us all in the face. But it's no good relying on the TV or 'devices'. Stories are about connection, person-to-person connection. They are about inspiring us all with a sense of discovery and a love of the world about us. They are also about enabling us as individual people to develop a sense of our own inner selves. To develop a strategy to enable all this to happen is to engage in one of the most exciting and rewarding tasks that can be imagined.

GIANT CHILDREN

A new boy had arrived in the reception class which I'd visited several times before. You couldn't fail to notice him: noticeably bigger than the rest of the group, he had a smilingly amiable face. He'd only been in the class a week or two but he already seemed quite at home there.

When the class sat down for stories, he sat at the front at one side and throughout he looked up attentively as, arm raised to represent the road in the tale, I told *Little Bear and the Long Road.*

Now we were at the crux of it. Little Bear had reached the end of the road and was looking down over the edge of the cliff (represented by the end of my fingers) as I enquired, 'What do you think Little Bear could see?'

The big new boy replied without hesitation. Looking up into my eyes as if I myself was Little Bear looking down at him, he gave a big smile and said, 'Giant children'.

9

CONSOLIDATING

Storytime is vital for children – which is why it's so important to make the whole experience as enjoyable as possible for them. But that enjoyment should never be just for them. It's vital for the adults who are involved as well. Preparing it, doing it, listening to responses: enjoying a task we see as worthwhile is a major motivator for us all.

But as I've acknowledged throughout this book, story-reading and storytelling with young children is not always the easiest thing to do. It can be difficult to organise, difficult to manage. Sometimes, it can also feel repetitive, like something you're doing because it's part of the routine in your particular setting or your home, something that's always got to be done. Yet if you place your focus on the children, storytime can come alive. Has one of your young listeners ever said to you, with feeling, 'That's the best story I ever heard'? Has a child who doesn't normally respond leaned forward and, amazingly, actually spoken during your storytime? Has a child later picked up on a story you've done and told it back to you in his or her own way? Have you seen a child's face brighten in the course of a story, seen that light coming into his or her eyes?

The educational and social value of doing stories with young children is well acknowledged. Yet in my view it's the direct response of the children that can best motivate us adults to keep on doing it or wanting to do it better. This is where reading about it comes in too. Descriptions of the experience by other people can help us in any number of ways. They can provide reassurance by making us realise we're on the right tracks. They can encourage us to try out new techniques and different approaches. They can make us feel we're not isolated in what we're trying to do but taking part in an important human endeavour.

So I want to refer here to three books I have personally found especially stimulating when trying to put my thoughts on doing stories with children into a wider context. Each of them emphasises the kind of collaboration – between adults working in a centre, between adults working in a centre and parents, and between adults and children – that I have tried to recommend throughout this present book. To me, it is establishing common bonds through stories that creates successful story work with early years children and, through doing this, establishes a firm basis for the development of the children's language and imagination.

First to mention is a book that was originally published in 1990 by an American early years teacher and education researcher, Vivian Gussin Paley. By now *The Boy Who Would Be a Helicopter* has become a worldwide classic. It presents the very particular use of storytelling its author introduced into her own early years classroom. Always present in the background is the story-reading and oral telling of stories that was regularly done with the children. In the foreground, and providing a fascinating story that focuses on one small boy, is the method the author developed of enabling stories the children produced themselves to be heard every day and in such a way that it became part of their social and intellectual development as human beings.

Two different areas of the classroom are of central importance in Vivian Gussin Paley's practice as she describes it. One is the story table in what she calls the story room. Here children can come on an individual basis to tell her a story that is in their heads. As she listens to the story, she scribes it on a piece of paper which then becomes the child's to use and to keep. The other important area in the story room is a taped square in the centre of the room which, at some point every day, becomes a kind of stage where, with the help of other children in the classroom, a child can act out the story he or she has created.

An immediate lesson from what happens in her way of working is that children's own stories are rarely stories in the sense we adults may expect. For many of us, including many educators, the stories she records from her classroom would probably not register as full stories at all. Educators tend to insist on beginnings and middles and ends. These stories are short, sometimes very short, sometimes consisting of just one line. For instance, one story that is quoted was told by a three-year-old called Vinnie, who was hugging her teddy bear upside down at the time. Vinnie simply said, 'There was a bear that he standed on his head.' A longer story told by a boy called Simon was about squirrels and it was one of many stories he used to tell on this theme: 'Once there was a little squirrel. And his mother said, "Go sleep in a waterbed." So he did. And he drowned inside. And he got not-drownded because it leaked out and he leaked out. The mother told him to swim home. But he couldn't swim.'

Another useful lesson is that children may have more in their minds than they're able to express. With gentle prompting, they may be able to say more. At the story table in

Vivian Gussin Paley's classroom, the adult scribing a child's story may frequently intervene to check that she or he has heard it aright or to ask a question. Such interventions are a way of taking seriously what a child has said and not simply assuming that something which does not make immediate sense is nothing but nonsense. In the case of Simon's squirrel story, for instance, Vivian Gussin Paley asked him, 'How does the little squirrel get home, Simon? As he can't swim.' The child replied, 'It wasn't an ocean. It was just a stream. So he walked home.'

Vivian Gussin Paley's book recognises that it can take a long time and considerable patience to enable a child to communicate at all, let alone in a way that relates to others. The boy whose fascination with helicopters provides her title demonstrates quite how much patience can be needed. By means of the story processes used in her classroom, this particular boy gradually changed from being an extremely isolated figure who not only did not interact with other children but often got in their way, bumping into them and disturbing their play, whirling round the room making helicopter noises. For weeks and months, all he'd say was that his wings were broken and he had to fix them. But with time and patience, he first became able to show an interest in participating in other children's story enactments and finally was able to share his own helicopter obsession, incorporating himself and his story into the other children's stories and their stories into his.

I guess there wouldn't be a majority of early years staff who would wish to or could choose to adopt Vivian Gussin Paley's method to the full extent she describes. But the approach should be illuminating for us all. It not only offers an important corrective to what many of us may regard as a story by showing the futility, where young children are concerned, of insisting on such aspects as appropriate endings and grammatical correctness. It also shows how children may be underestimated. They may have far more in their mind than they're able to express. With gentle prompting, they might be able to say more.

My next book to mention is by Trisha Lee, an English story worker and a convinced practitioner of Vivian Gussin Paley's methods. In 2002 she founded the theatre and education company MakeBelieve Arts to develop the creative potential of children across the age spectrum from early years to secondary. In *Princesses, Dragons and Helicopter Stories*, published in 2016, she sets out how she has used and developed Vivian Gussin Paley's methods. With her meticulous description of every step in the process, you would feel extremely well supported if you wished to use it to try out the method either in whole or in part. But it's what comes across about Trisha Lee's approach to talking to children that makes her book so well worth reading by anyone involved in early years work.

Too often in an early years setting, a member of staff can feel pressurised by the amount of stuff that has to be done. In such circumstances, it can be all too easy to become confrontational with a child who is being a pain. Examples of how another experienced adult approaches such problems can give helpful pause for thought. As Trisha Lee describes it, her personal practice resists imposing instructions and demands on the children. If a child is acting up, she instead might say, 'I have a problem about understanding what you want to do. Would you like to tell me?' At the same time, there are clear rules. These respect the child as a thinking and feeling human being and are seen as applying to the adults as much as to the children.

To sum up some of the most useful points in Trisha Lee's book:

- It understands that you can't oblige children to learn things: they have to sort things out for themselves.

- It realises the extent to which literacy is not a matter of teaching phonics and grammar, but engaging children's interest and imagination and finding ways to relate to their own inner stories.

- It gives space to the kind of stories and responses to stories that come from children even when these may not look like proper stories to some adults coming across them for the first time.

- Perhaps most instructive of all, it explains how observing an adult actually writing with pen or pencil and paper makes the act of writing come to life for children. Seeing their own words being written down enables them to see a point in learning to write. It makes them want to do it too.

Through all these positive points, Trisha Lee gives real insight into how to work with children in such a way as to bring out their ideas. An added plus is an especially interesting section on dealing with the obsession some children develop with guns or fighting or superheroes. Banning it doesn't work. What are you to do instead? The book gives specific advice within the context of the story scribing, story acting method.

The third book I want to mention deals with both story-reading and storytelling. Its author, Bob Barton, is a convinced believer in the value of both. His own wide experience backs up his belief. A co-founder of the renowned Storytellers School of Toronto, he has also been a teacher and it is evident how much he enjoys giving thought to ways of bringing stories to life and involving listeners in them. *Telling Stories Your Way* (2000) conveys a great deal about his approach. Throughout, its emphasis is on what each of us as individuals can bring to stories, whether through reading aloud or telling. He also shows how in preparing and delivering stories, all of us do not only draw on our own personal resources. We develop these in the process.

While the applicable age range of Bob Barton's book is considerably wider than early years – it goes right up to college level – it begins with an area of central interest for early years children, namely nursery rhymes. Indeed, it was the author's developing love for these – their strong, driving rhythms on the one hand, their humour and quirkiness on the other – that first got him involved in oral storytelling. Questions he began to ask himself about how nursery rhymes originated led him to all kinds of myths and folk tales. Thinking about these in turn – and especially about how to tell them with his students – enabled him to begin discovering what he describes as 'new ways to release print from the pages of books' (p.17).

Releasing print from the pages of books is what this book of mine has been about too. Whether we're reading or telling, it's that freeing of the story to make it our own that all of us have to achieve if we're to give stories the energy that will result in engaging others in them. Bob Barton gives good advice about what this means. On the question of selecting a story, for instance, he affirms the crucial point that stories are a very personal matter, whether for reading aloud or telling. You have to choose ones that you like. 'You find yourself sifting through dozens of stories in order to find one that appeals to you' (p.19). This can involve a lot of effort. Then there's a second stage. Through actually doing the story you find out why you like it – or not.

Like me, Bob Barton believes the activity of preparing stories is vital. For people wanting to try oral telling, he makes the useful point that stories in the oral tradition are inclined to provide their own help: traditional stories have built-in tricks of rhythm, rhyme and repetition that are, in themselves, aids to memory. Yet absorbing a story for oral telling is not and can never be a matter of memorising it word by word. You have to work out the structure of the story, become familiar with its bones and in the process get it into your head in your own words. Then you have to tell it to yourself again and again. You might retell it silently. You might retell it aloud to yourself or a friend or a partner. Whatever your preferred approach, it's your own words and the natural rhythms of those words that you need to be finding and feeling. The work involved is what frees the story from other people's tellings and retellings of it. And it's that freeing of the story that enables you to take possession of it. It's what makes it become your own. But beware, warns Bob Barton. Openings and closings are extremely important. 'A bit of raggedness in the middle won't matter much, but an uncertain start or a muddled conclusion don't make for a satisfying listening experience. Even though you will continue to shape and reshape the story as you practise it, try to keep beginnings and endings well-polished' (p.51).

Telling Stories Your Way is equally proactive in its approach to story-reading. It's Bob Barton's belief that listening to a story being read aloud can give children all they need for bringing the story alive in their minds: 'the storyteller's pacing, intonation, gestures, and expression support their efforts to "think the pictures"' (p.18). As this happens, the listener becomes an active participant in the re-creation of the story. But reading a story aloud should never be regarded as the easy option. As much as for the oral teller, the job is to bring the story to life and this necessitates preparation. It means getting a prior knowledge of the story's characters and events and the thoughts and feelings they may produce. As with oral telling, visualisation is key. So too is becoming specifically aware of the text to be read and how it flows across the book's pages, as well as of when to turn the pages to build up suspense and realising when a bit of pruning of the text may be needed. Most importantly, it means becoming aware of the rhythms in the text so these can be properly conveyed in the sounds and textures of the story reader's voice.

As to those strange or difficult words that may come up in a story we've selected, it's Bob Barton's good advice that using any such word within the context of the story will suffice to make its meaning understood. He is also quite sure of the value of not dismissing difficult words: 'words not understood have a charm and magic of their own which children enjoy' (p.71). Puzzling over them can be fun, as can listening to their sound and guessing at what they might mean.

Covering all ages from early years to college students, *Telling Stories Your Way* obviously goes way beyond the age group that is the focus of this present book of mine. But for some readers, its very width of perspective might prove helpful. Showing the applicability of stories from the earliest years, it makes abundantly clear why, from the very beginning, it is so important to provide encouragement and space for children to express themselves. Later in their education, the ability to do this will become vital. So a collaborative approach makes sense from the very beginning. It's why Bob Barton believes in allowing and enabling children to chime in, why he believes in creating a nurturing environment where the sharing of people's ideas of story is something that happens regularly, why he believes in inviting children to retell the stories they're given in their own way. These beliefs have educational value. If pupils at later ages are expected to be able to create, interpret and explore, doesn't it make sense to introduce such processes from the very beginning?

PARTNERSHIP AND COLLABORATION

I profoundly agree. Stories are very important. They are important to our education. They are important to our emotional health and they are important to our ability to socialise with others. Stories appeal to our deepest feelings. Often they reach areas of our being that lie deeper than any words we can find to express them. Even as they do that, they can help us to understand ourselves, each other and the world around us. They have importance on an individual level.

At the same time, it's also true that stories are very communal things. Through the sharing of them, we come to know the extent to which our own feelings and experiences are common to others. Stories can enable us to feel less alone. They can give us the sense of being part of a human continuum. Through stories, we may find ourselves identifying with human beings who, it's clear from the story, lived a very long time ago or in a significantly different culture from ours. Through stories, we may find ourselves understanding more about the conflicts of today. Stories have importance on an interpersonal level.

In this book I've argued for all kinds of collaboration in the business of dealing with these extraordinarily powerful things we call stories. Collaboration between the different members of early years teams can have the effect of making everyone feel more supported and more purposeful. Collaboration between the parents of early years children and those who work with them can bring about a real sharing of the pleasure of stories as well as more knowledge of their effects. But most of all, I've argued for treating the telling and reading of stories to children as a collaboration between the adults who do it and the children to whom they offer it. In a very real and honest way, creating such a partnership puts everyone involved on the same level. Try it out if you haven't already. What results in terms of response can be so beguiling you'll never again want to do it any other way.

Appendix 1

Stories and Rhymes

CHAPTER 2

Doctor Foster went to Gloucester
In a shower of rain.
He fell in a puddle right up to his middle
And never went there again.

A DARK, DARK TALE

Once upon a time there was a dark, dark moor.

On the dark, dark moor was a dark, dark path.

Along the dark, dark path was a dark, dark wall.

In the dark, dark wall was a dark, dark gate.

Behind the dark, dark gate was a dark, dark garden.

In the dark, dark garden was a dark, dark house.

In the dark, dark house was a dark, dark door.

Behind the dark, dark door was a dark, dark staircase.

Up the dark, dark staircase was a dark, dark room.

In the dark, dark room was a dark, dark chest.

In the dark, dark chest, can you guess what there was?

Note: it's a little mouse that's in the chest at the end of Ruth Brown's *A Dark, Dark Tale*. But you can get other wonderful responses if you ask the children. Plus, you can make the journey all over again, only this time make it a different journey, perhaps from a dark, dark forest down a dark, dark hole beneath a tree.

MRS WIGGLE AND MRS WAGGLE

Note: This action chant needs you to use your fists and your thumbs. Each closed fist represents a house with a closed door. Open your fist to open the door. Raise your thumb to show a person going out of the door. Then, for Mrs Wiggle's journey or Mrs Waggle's journey, move your right or left thumb up and down in an arc to represent going up, over and down the three hills.

Part 1

One day, Mrs Wiggle woke up in the morning and said, 'I'm going to see my friend.'

＊So Mrs Wiggle got ready. Then she went out of the door and set off.

She went

Up the hill and down the hill

Up the hill and down the hill

Up the hill and down the hill

Until she came to Mrs Waggle's house.

When she got there, she knocked on the door. No answer.

She knocked again. No answer. 'Where can Mrs Waggle be?'

She called through the letter-box: 'Mrs Waggle, where are you?'

No answer. So Mrs Wiggle went home.

(Repeat the 'Up the hill and down the hill' refrain, changing the last line to 'Until she got home'.)

When Mrs Wiggle got home, she went in her house and had a nice cup of tea and a biscuit. Then she went to bed. *Yawn**

Part 2

Next morning, Mrs Waggle woke up and said, 'I'm going to see my friend.'

Now, with the appropriate name change, repeat the chant from * to *.

Part 3

Next morning, Mrs Wiggle and Mrs Waggle both woke up at the same time and said, 'I'm going to see my friend.' So each of them went out of their house and set off.

Now do a bit of a double act, using both your thumbs while you do the first part of the refrain:

Up the hill and down the hill

Up the hill and...

(And as the two women meet on top of the second hill, so your thumbs will meet and there will be great hugs and kisses and exclamations of delight and, if you wish, exchange of news.)

Then Mrs Wiggle and Mrs Waggle set off home: 'Bye bye. See you later.'

(Use your thumbs again to see them home, and at this point, say that both will have a cup of tea and go to bed.)

And in bed, before going to sleep, both of them said the same thing at the same time.

'Isn't it nice to have a friend?'

TWO ACTION CHANTS

The Sea Chant

The sea is deep, the sea is wide.
The sea's got lots of things inside.
It's got...? Fishes...

The Forest Chant

The forest is deep, the forest is wide.
The forest's got lots of things inside.
It's got...? Trees...

How to do them

1. Start by chanting the rhyme in a loud, clear voice with accompanying hand gestures as follows: Line 1, hands moving down in front of you to suggest depth, then moving out wide to suggest width; Line 2, hands and shoulders suggesting abundance; Line 3, hands inviting response.

2. First time round, answer your own question, 'It's got...?' by suggesting, for example, that the sea has got fishes. Make a hand action to represent the fishes.

3. Second time round, repeat your own suggestion (i.e. fishes) and, looking expectantly round, invite your listeners to come up with another idea. Ask whoever responds if they've got an action to go with it. If they're too shy, ask someone else to volunteer one on their behalf.

4. Third time round and on each subsequent occasion, add each new idea and its accompanying gesture so that the chant gets longer and longer.

THE TIGER AND THE MOUSE

Once there was a little mouse. One day the mouse was going along in the forest when, all of a sudden, she heard a loud roar. There in front of her was a tiger.

'Ha!' said the tiger. 'You got in my way so I'm going to eat you up. I could do with a snack.'

The mouse was frightened. Her heart started thumping. But the little mouse had brains.

'No,' said the mouse. 'Don't eat me up. For if you eat me, I'll never be able to help you.'

'Help me?' said the tiger, astonished. 'You are only a little mouse. I'm a big strong tiger. How could you ever help me?'

'I don't know yet,' said the little mouse. 'But if you spare me, I'll look out for you and give you my help if ever you need it.'

'Huh,' said the tiger. 'I don't believe you. But I'll give you a chance just this once. And if you don't help me, I'll come and find you and then I'll eat you up.'

One day not long after that, some big bad hunters came into the forest. They were looking for tigers to catch. And they caught the tiger that had spared the mouse. When they'd caught him, they tied him with ropes and left him in the forest while they went for their truck. They knew what they were going to do: they were going to sell the tiger for a lot of money.

While the hunters were away, the little mouse was going through the forest. Suddenly she heard a loud, sad roar. When she followed the sound, she saw the tiger was trapped. His legs were tied so he couldn't move and the hunters had pegged him to the ground.

The mouse ran across to the tiger. 'Don't worry,' she said. 'I'll help you. I'll keep the promise I made.'

'How can you help me?' said the tiger. 'The hunters have caught me and I can't get away.'

'Just wait,' the little mouse said, 'and you'll soon see what I can do.'

At once, the little mouse started nibbling away at the ropes. Soon she had eaten through them all and the tiger was free.

'Thank you,' the tiger said to the mouse. 'You kept your word and from this day on, I promise I'll always be your friend.'

CHAPTER 3

NURSERY RHYMES

I'll tell you a story about Jackanory
And now my story's begun.
I'll tell you another
About Jack and his brother
And now my story is done.

Little Miss Myrtle sat on a turtle
Thinking it was a chair.
'Ow-ee!' said the turtle.
'I'm sorry,' said Myrtle,
'But I didn't know you were there.'

There was a maid on Scrabble Hill
And if not dead, she lives there still.
She grew so tall, she touched the sky
And on the moon hung clothes to dry.

There are men in the village of Erith
Whom nobody seeth or heareth
And there looms on the marge
Of the river, a barge
That nobody roweth or steereth.

On Saturday night I lost my wife
And where do you think I found her?
Up in the moon, singing a tune
With all the stars around her.

CHAPTER 4

LITTLE RED MONKEY

Retold by Mary Medlicott from the picture book by John Astrop (2010).

The little red monkey was always up to tricks. As he went round the jungle, he'd be singing his song: 'La, la, la, la! What shall I do today, I wonder?' But he'd be looking for mischievous things to do.

One day, he painted pink spots all over the hippo's back. The hippo was very cross: 'Who painted these spots on my back?'

Another day, he tied the elephant's trunk in a knot. The elephant could hardly speak: 'Who tied this dot in my twunk?'

Another day, he pulled the parrot's tail. The parrot squawked: 'Who's pulling my tail?'

Another day, when all the little animals were having their afternoon sleep, he got out his drums and banged them loudly. The little animals woke up, crying: 'Who's waking us up from our afternoon sleep?'

In the end, the animals of the jungle became very cross. They gathered together to discuss what to do. 'What shall we do about that little red monkey? We've got to teach him a lesson.'

They came up with lots of different ideas (your children might have quite a few!) and in the end they decided. First, they'd dig a deep hole in the jungle. Then, because monkeys like to eat bananas, they'd collect bananas from the trees (children could count how many) and they'd fill the deep hole with all the bananas. Then the little red monkey would come along and eat them and, as he ate, he'd sink into the hole. Then they'd have him trapped.

When they were ready, the animals hid and waited.

Soon the little red monkey came along. 'Aha, bananas, my favourite!' After jumping on top of the bananas, the little red monkey started eating them up. As he ate each one, he tossed away the skin and he was so busy eating that he didn't notice that, as he ate, he sank lower and lower in the hole.

Before long, he was at the bottom. When he saw that, he tried to jump out. But he couldn't. The hole was too deep. He was very upset. 'Help!' he called out. 'I'm stuck in a hole. Please come and get me out.'

Well, the animals came to the top of the hole and looked down at the little red monkey. Then they discussed the question. Shall we get him out? In the end, they decided they would. But how? (Again, your children might have some ideas!)

In the end, the elephant put his trunk down into the hole, the monkey grabbed it and the elephant pulled him out. The little red monkey said, 'Thank you, I'll be good from now on.'

And what do you think? Indeed, he was good and kind. He scrubbed the paint spots off the hippo's back, he untied the knot in the elephant's trunk, he smoothed the parrot's tail and he played nice music in the afternoons to help the little animals to go to sleep.

The little red monkey still goes round the jungle singing his song: 'La, la, la, la! What shall I do today, I wonder?' But nowadays, he's always looking for nice things to do.

The end

A HOUSE FOR ME

There was once a boy who wanted a house. So he set off to try and find one.

He walked and he walked and he walked. And after a while he came to a big pile of earth. As he went past, he heard a voice: 'Where are you going, my friend?' When the boy looked, he saw a worm wriggling its way out of the earth.

'I'm looking for a house for me,' said the boy. 'Well,' said the worm, 'you should come and live with me. This pile of earth is warm and snug. Come with me and have a look.' 'All right,' said the boy and followed the worm. But it was too dark in that pile of earth and pieces of earth trickled down the boy's neck. He didn't like it at all. 'I can't live here,' the boy said to the worm. 'It's a nice place for you but not for me.' So the boy wriggled out and went on his way.

He walked and he walked and he walked. And after a while he came to a river. As he went past, he heard a voice: 'Where are you going, my friend?' When the boy looked, he saw a fish peering out of the water. 'I'm looking for a house for me,' said the boy. 'Well,' said the fish, 'come and live in my river. There's plenty of room and it's nice and cool.' 'All right,' said the boy and he jumped in the river. But the water felt cold and he couldn't swim very well. He didn't like it at all. 'I can't live here,' said the boy to the fish. 'It's a nice place for you but not for me.' So the boy climbed out and walked on.

He walked and he walked and he walked. And after a while he came to a tree. As he went past, he heard a voice: 'Where are you going, my friend?' When the boy looked up, he saw a bird in the tree. 'I'm looking for a house for me,' said the boy. 'Well,' said the bird, 'you should come and live here. There's an excellent view and a nice cool breeze.' 'All right,' said the boy. 'I'll come and see.' So he climbed up into the tree. But as he got near the top, he felt very dizzy. He didn't like it at all. 'I can't live here,' said the boy to the bird. 'It's nice for you but not for me.' So he climbed down and went on his way.

He walked and he walked and he walked. And after a while he came to a wall. As he went past, he heard a voice: 'Where are you going, my young friend?' When the boy looked, he saw a builder the other side of the wall. 'I'm looking for a house for me,' said the boy. 'Well,' said the builder, 'you should stay right here. I know about making houses and if you help me finish this one, I'll help you make one of your own.' So the boy helped the builder to finish his house and then the builder helped the boy to make one of his own. When it was finished, the boy moved in and the builder gave him a present. It was his very own front-door key. The boy felt happy and pleased. He said, 'This is the best place in the world for me.'

The end

(But there can be some interesting discussion here at the end. Did that boy live in his new house on his own? Some people think that what he did was go back to the old house where he lived before to fetch his family to come and live in the new one.)

LITTLE BEAR AND THE LONG ROAD

Note: Before telling this story, provide yourself with a little bear and before starting the tale, bring him out and say some nice things about him, including that his mummy loves him and always watches out for him.

The journey out

Little Bear loved going out.

At the end of his gate was a very long road. (Raise one arm and stretch it out level in front of you to represent the road.)

On this particular day, Little Bear decided he'd go to the end of the road. So he set off. (Walking sounds are needed here, e.g. Tumpety, tumpety, tumpety, tump.)

Soon he came to a big, steep hill. (Raise your arm, elbow pointing upwards to represent the hill.)

'I'll get up that hill,' Little Bear said to himself. (Sounds of effort are a good idea as Little Bear ascends your arm, e.g. Rumpety, tumpety, HEAVE. Rumpety, tumpety, HEAVE.)

When Little Bear got to the top, he was pleased. He said, 'Now I can slide down the other side.'

So that's what Little Bear did. (Accompany his slide with appropriate sounds, e.g. Wheeeeeee!)

At the bottom of the hill, Little Bear carried on walking. (Tumpety, tumpety, tumpety, tump.)

Soon he came to a river. (If you're wearing a watch or bracelet, this can represent the river where Little Bear must pause. If not, simply point to your wrist.)

'I think I'll jump,' Little Bear said. (Little Bear must now make a huge big jump with accompanying very loud sounds, e.g. 1...2...3...J-U-M-P!)

Then Little Bear continued his journey till he came to the end of the road. (By now, Little Bear has moved to the end of your fingers and seems to be looking down. An astonished cry is needed: Wow!)

And do you know what Little Bear saw when he looked? (Here it's time for suggestions from your audience or, if there are none from them, from you: A big wide sea? A big sandy beach? A dark forest? Another little bear down below?)

And what do you think happened then? (Your choice. Perhaps Little Bear goes down to explore. Perhaps he simply enjoys the view before realising it's time to go home.)

The journey home

The return journey must mirror the outward journey – same features, same noises but faster.

When Little Bear reaches home, there must be something to eat or drink and also an opportunity to tell the story of his journey to his mummy. This is the storyteller's opportunity to quickly recapitulate the story before putting Little Bear away or letting him visit his audience.

Appendix 2

Classic Stories and Picture Books

Ten classic picture books for story-reading

Mr Gumpy's Outing by John Burningham

Where the Wild Things Are by Maurice Sendak

Mr Magnolia by Quentin Blake

Funny Bones by Janet and Allan Ahlberg

Room on the Broom by Julia Donaldson

We're Going on a Bear Hunt by Michael Rosen

The Tiger Who Came to Tea by Judith Kerr

Peace at Last by Jill Murphy

Where's Spot? by Eric Hill

Ten classic tales for telling

Note: versions of all the tales below are available on the internet, including as YouTube animations and tellings.

The Enormous Turnip

The Elves and the Shoemaker

The Gingerbread Man

Goldilocks and the Three Bears

Jack and the Beanstalk

Little Red Riding Hood

The Little Red Hen

The Magic Porridge Pot

The Three Little Pigs

Rumpelstiltskin

Picture-book tales from different lands

The Tiger Child – a folk tale from India, by Joanna Troughton

Pattan's Pumpkin – a flood story from Kerala, India, by Chitra Soundar

The Crow's Tale – a Lenni Lenape Native American Legend, by Naomi Howarth

Deep in the Woods – a Russian folk tale, by Christopher Corr

Bringing the Rain to Kapiti Plain – a tale from Kenya, by Verna Aardema

The Leopard's Drum – an Asante tale from West Africa, by Jessica Souhami

Abiyoyo – a folk tale from South Africa, by Pete Seeger

Tiddalick, the Greedy Frog – an Aboriginal Dreamtime story, by Nicholas Wu

Where the Forest Meets the Sea – a discovery tale about North Queensland, Australia, by Jeannie Baker

The Great Race – the story of the Chinese Zodiac, by Dawn Casey

Bibliography

References

Astrop, John (1978) *Little Red Monkey*. London: Hutchinson.

Barton, Bob (2000) *Telling Stories Your Way: Storytelling and Reading Aloud in the Classroom*. Markham, ON: Pembroke Publishers Limited.

Blackman, Malorie (2012) '21st century storytelling: Will the advent of new technology create a paradigm shift in the writing and reading of children's literature?' *The Philippa Pearce Lecture*. Available at www.pearcelecture.com/the-lectures/2012-2 (accessed 8 November 2017).

Brown, Ruth (1983) *A Dark, Dark Tale*. Witney: Scholastic Publications.

Butler, Dorothy (1980) *Babies Need Books*. London: The Bodley Head.

Campbell, Joseph (1988) *The Power of Myth*. New York, NY: Doubleday.

Carle, Eric (1969) *The Very Hungry Caterpillar*. New York, NY: World Publishing Company.

Colwell, Eileen (1980) *Storytelling*. London: The Bodley Head.

Crace, Jim (2001) 'Book Talk.' *Bookforum Magazine*, Fall.

Foreman, Michael (1993) *Dinosaurs and All That Rubbish*. London: Puffin Books.

Lee, Trisha (2016) *Princesses, Dragons and Helicopter Stories: Storytelling and Story Acting in the Early Years*. Abingdon: Routledge.

Minns, Hilary (1990) *Read It to Me Now: Learning at Home and at School*. London: Virago Press.

Paley, Vivian Gussin (1990) *The Boy Who Would Be a Helicopter: The Uses of Storytelling in the Classroom*. Cambridge, MA: Harvard University Press.

Rosen, Betty (1991) *Shapers and Polishers: Teachers as Storytellers*. Kingston upon Thames: Mary Glasgow Publications.

Rosen, Michael (1989) *We're Going on a Bear Hunt*. London: Walker Books.

Seeger, Pete (1987) *Abiyoyo*. London: Hamish Hamilton.

Shedlock, Marie (1951) *The Art of the Story-Teller*. Mineola, NY: Dover Publications (originally published 1915).

Snow, Jon (2016) 'I lived in some fear of my father.' *The Guardian*, 30 December. Available at www.theguardian.com/lifeandstyle/2016/dec/30/jon-snow-i-lived-in-some-fear-of-my-father-boarding-school-being-bullied (accessed 8 November 2017).

Useful websites and organisations

For story resources
Book Trust: www.booktrust.org.uk
Early Learning HQ: www.earlylearninghq.org.uk
Literacy Trust: www.literacytrust.org.uk
British Council Learn English Kids:
www.learnenglishkids.britishcouncil.org

For information on storytelling and storytellers
Society for Storytelling: www.sfs.org.uk
Scottish Storytelling Centre: www.tracscotland.org
Verbal Arts Centre (Londonderry): www.theverbal.co

Previous books by Mary Medlicott include
(2010) *Stories for Young Children and How to Tell Them!* (Includes CD) London: A&C Black.
(2003; 2nd edition 2014) *The Little Book of Storytelling*. London: Bloomsbury Publishing.

Index